Also by Jen Petro-Roy

P.S. I Miss You

Good Enough

Life in the Balance

YOU ARE ENOUGH

JEN PETRO-ROY

SQUARE
FISH

Feiwel and Friends

New York

The information in this book is not intended to replace the advice of the reader's own physician or other medical professional. You should consult a medical professional in matters relating to health, especially if you have existing medical conditions, and before starting, stopping, or changing the dose of any medication you are taking. Individual readers are solely responsible for their own health care decisions. The author and the publisher do not accept responsibility for any adverse effects individuals may claim to experience, whether directly or indirectly, from the information contained in this book.

The fact that an organization or website is mentioned in the book as a potential source of information does not mean that the author or the publisher endorse any of the information they may provide or recommendations they may make.

SQUARE
FISH

An imprint of Macmillan Publishing Group, LLC
120 Broadway, New York, NY 10271
mackids.com

Square Fish and the Square Fish logo are trademarks of Macmillan and
are used by Feiwel and Friends under license from Macmillan.

Our books may be purchased in bulk for promotional, educational, or business use. Please
contact your local bookseller or the Macmillan Corporate and Premium Sales Department at
(800) 221-7945 ext. 5442 or by email at MacmillanSpecialMarkets@macmillan.com.

Library of Congress Cataloging-in-Publication Data
Names: Petro-Roy, Jen, author.
Title: You are enough / Jen Petro-Roy.
Description: New York, NY : Feiwel and Friends, [2019] | Audience: 9–12. | Includes bibliographical
references.
Identifiers: LCCN 2018019396 | ISBN 978-1-250-15101-8 (paperback) |
ISBN 978-1-250-15100-1 (ebook)
Subjects: LCSH: Eating disorders in adolescence—Psychological aspects—Juvenile literature. |
Eating disorders in adolescence—Treatment—Juvenile literature. | Body image in adolescence—
Juvenile literature.
Classification: LCC RC552.E18 P47 2019 | DDC 616.85/2600835—dc23
LC record available at https://lccn.loc.gov/2018019396

Originally published in the United States by Feiwel and Friends
First Square Fish edition, 2021
Book designed by Rebecca Syracuse
Square Fish logo designed by Filomena Tuosto

1 3 5 7 9 10 8 6 4 2

To Ellie and Lucy.
You are everything. I love you.

TABLE OF CONTENTS

PART TWO: TOOLS AND INFORMATION FOR RECOVERY

HOW TO USE THIS BOOK

IN THE INTRODUCTION to this book, I discuss a bit about my own struggles with an eating disorder, and my journey to body acceptance. As you read, please keep in mind that I am writing about my experience alone, about my thoughts and my body alone. In a similar situation, others may have reacted in a different way. The way I related to food and dealt with an eating disorder is no more or less valid than anyone else's.

I am not a medical professional. I do not have experience with every single way food and self-esteem can affect someone's life. The introduction will touch upon my limitations and the ways I worked to fill in the gaps to make this book as helpful to as many different people and populations as possible.

Part One of this book will discuss eating disorders themselves. What are eating disorders? Who gets them? What other factors can be involved that might make recovery harder? How are eating disorders different from what the media often shows us?

Part Two of this book will discuss different skills and pieces of information that were crucial to *my* recovery, pieces that I hope you can apply to your life through the exercises included at the end of many chapters.

Part Three will cover common situations that you may face while struggling to recover, especially when it comes to people and situations that can seem out of your control (society, friends, family, the media), and will discuss how to combat the bad body image that may accompany your steps forward.

Part Four will talk about what needs to change (both in you and in your environment) as you recover—what steps you may need to take and what boundaries you may need to set up to best guard the way you are learning to feel about your one unique and wonderful self.

The back of the book contains additional resources and source notes, information on scholarship funds for treatment, and recommended books and websites. You can look at this as you are reading or after; it's up to you!

The chapters and subject headings are set up to allow you to skip around the book. If you think a segment in Part

Three will really help you with the place you're in, you can read that section first, without taking away from the message of the rest of the book.

As you read, remember that some people get their eating disorders recognized early while others are never identified. Some families can afford hospital stays and residential treatment, while others struggle with the costs of therapy.

People struggling with eating disorders can be any weight. (I don't like to use the term "normal weight," because what even *is* normal?)

Many people think they don't deserve or need treatment, and some "eating issues" are labeled "not severe enough" for treatment.

Every experience is different, just as every personality and every body is different. The common thread, though, is that we all deserve recovery. No matter your height or weight or body shape or size, no matter what behaviors or thoughts you struggle with, you deserve to recover. You deserve to accept yourself and like yourself and (yes!) even love yourself.

This book is for you. I want it to help you. That's because *you* are important. *You* deserve to read this message and apply these lessons to *your* life.

Let's get started.

A NOTE ABOUT LANGUAGE

FIRST OF ALL, I want to emphasize that language, including terms used to describe specific populations, is always changing. Words that were once seen as insults are now embraced and new words are always being added. For many groups, certain terms can be contentious, embraced by some and rejected by others. Throughout this book, I did the best I could to use terms that would be as clear and welcoming as possible. However, it is possible that some people will have a problem with words I use in this book, and two in particular:

1. QUEER

Queer is a term with a long and complicated history: It's been used as a slur, but it's also been used in an academic sense and as an identity. Some lesbian, gay, bisexual, transgender, intersex, asexual, aromantic, or pansexual (LGBTQIAP) people also identify as queer, and some don't. Some people feel comfortable using queer as an umbrella term, some prefer an acronym like LGBTQIAP+ or something else.

After listening to a number of people who identify as queer and/or LGBTQIAP+, I've decided to use queer as an umbrella term for a group of people including those who identify as lesbian, gay, bisexual, transgender, nonbinary, questioning, asexual, aromantic, and pansexual.

2. FAT

Fat is another complicated word. Many people see *fat* as an insult and a cruel thing to call someone. However, like *queer, fat* has been reclaimed by fat acceptance activists who embrace the word *fat* and encourage others to use it in a descriptive, positive, or neutral way. Many people prefer it to terms like *overweight* or *obese*, but not everyone does. While some people find the word *fat* empowering, many others still find it hurtful.

That being said, after listening to fat activists, I believe that using the term *fat* rather than *overweight* or *obese* is the most respectful thing to do. So when you see *fat* used throughout the book, know that I am using it as a descriptive term, not as a negative term, nor as a way to insult any group of people.

Also, please note that my use of *queer* and *fat* doesn't mean that all the people interviewed in this book would agree with my usage of the terms.

INTRODUCTION

My Journey

How it started

THERE WAS A VOICE in my head for twelve years. More than that, actually. It told me what I should eat and how long I should exercise. It told me that sleep made me lazy and that my body was a work of art I needed to perfect.

It told me that I *was* my body, that everything else about me—my interests, my family, my friends, and my health—didn't matter. All I had to do was be skinny and the world would fall into place.

It will be easy, the voice said. *It will be the best thing you'll ever do.*

There wasn't a *real* voice in my head, but it felt that way sometimes. My anxiety when I didn't listen to that voice felt real, too. The anxiety took over my body, making my stomach cramp and my head whirl and my body tense up. Every cell in my brain was devoted to worrying about my body and what I looked like.

I hated it. I loved it.

My eating disorder wasn't my first experience with anxiety or obsession. I had always been a high-strung child. I had friends and had fun and got dirty, but part of me was always worried about *something*:

How my socks didn't feel just right on my feet.

How someone I loved was going to die because I hadn't said "I love you" enough times before bed.

How my friends were just *pretending* to like me.

In sixth grade, a friend and I always joked that if we failed a quiz, it would mean we wouldn't know enough for the big test. If we failed that test, we wouldn't pass the grade. Then we wouldn't go on to high school or college, and we'd end up complete failures.

It was probably a joke to my friend, but it was reality to me. In my mind, every situation was a potential catastrophe. Every person could hurt me.

It wasn't a surprise when I was diagnosed with obsessive-compulsive disorder in the seventh grade. The repeated rituals and fear of cleaning products were pretty obvious signs. My parents hustled me into therapy, and I went on medication to help with my anxiety. After a while, a lot of my behaviors slowed down. My thoughts cleared enough so I could function better.

Back then, I wasn't very worried about my body. I thought about what clothes and shoes I should buy to fit in with my classmates (I thought about that a lot), but I didn't care much about the size I was wearing.

That would come later.

First came the realization that I was still anxious, when I started to prepare for high school and my friends staged an intervention because I was acting too "weird" for them.

I thought they were being mean. They were, of course, but what they didn't realize—what even I didn't yet realize—was that my "weirdness" was a manifestation of my anxiety. I was so afraid my friends didn't really like me that I was sabotaging every interaction we had, acting paranoid and trying too hard to be perfect.

My body issues would come in high school, when I joined the swim team and gained muscles, when my body went through the natural changes of adolescence, and when I broke down in sobs before the school Halloween dance. My friends and I had all dressed up as devils, and I was sure I was the fattest one. I was sure that fat was awful.

My eating disorder would come after I went to college, when I scrutinized my roommates the same way I did my hometown friends, searching for signs that they accepted me. I was so afraid I was boring and unlikable that I retreated into a world of food, weight, and exercise obsession. I thought that could help me avoid any potential rejection.

That's when the feelings of isolation took over and the disease began.

It all started in middle school, though:

My perfectionism.

My fear of not belonging.

My awareness of how I looked.

The anxiety that was always hovering in the background.

I wish I had caught it then. I wish I had reached out for help and admitted what was going on. I wish I knew that my body was not my enemy and that gaining weight isn't a bad thing.

That's what this book is for.

Whether you occasionally worry about your body or you're in the depths of an eating disorder.

Whether you think you might have some eating issues or you absolutely 100 percent know your life needs to change.

There's help out there for you, and there are lots of people who can help you. Taking that first step and talking to a guardian, school counselor, or therapist about how you feel can seem so difficult, but help and support *are* out there.

No matter where you are on your recovery journey, this book is for you. Because you deserve recovery. You deserve a life free from body worries and obsessions and compulsions and anxiety. You don't need an eating disorder.

You are enough just the way you are.

The journey, the fight

I spent one Christmas in the hospital. While the rest of my family was celebrating together, eating eagerly anticipated holiday treats, I was on the hospital ward, eating according to my meal plan and writing in my journal.

I wasn't supposed to be at the hospital. At that point, I had already been an inpatient for a few weeks, which meant that I was allowed a pass home for Christmas Eve and Christmas Day. I could sleep in my own bed instead of on the limp hospital mattress. I wouldn't have to follow the schedule that was the same every day: Get weighed, shower, eat. Therapy, support group, eat. Support group, nutrition appointment, eat. Eat, eat, and eat some more.

I was supposed to be excited to wake up in my bed on Christmas morning. I was supposed to be excited to open presents with my family and stare at the twinkling lights and talk about whatever "normal" people talk about in the presence of such overwhelming food.

I was not excited.

With every minute at home my anxiety rose, even though I was supposed to be getting "better." I had gained weight at the hospital. I had been eating the suggested meal plan for patients with anorexia for my entire stay, so these twenty-four hours at home were supposed to be easy. If I were a comedian, I'd make a food joke about everything being a piece of cake.

I was supposed to slide back into normalcy as an Olympic diver enters the water, with barely a splash or a ripple. I was supposed to be better now. If not all the way, then enough to enjoy Christmas the way everyone else was. I wasn't supposed to freak out at the amount my mother wanted me to eat. I wasn't supposed to be clenching my fists with anxiety the entire time.

Supposed to. Like *should*, it is a phrase that has tortured me for years. We all hear these words in some way. We all think them.

Here are some things I thought:

- Women are supposed to be thin, beautiful, and successful.
- Girls should behave and look nice, be confident but not *too* confident.
- Men are supposed to be muscular and toned.
- Boys should be athletic and popular and successful.

People are expected to fit neatly into categories, and these categories are often binary, with only two options, like woman or man. Girl or boy.

The world often forgets that people are all different. That people naturally come in all shapes and sizes. That boys get eating disorders, too. That gender isn't always binary. That trans people get eating disorders. That queer people get eating disorders. That fat people get eating disorders.

Anyone can have an eating disorder.

When I was younger, I definitely heard *should*s that pertained to me. I focused on the *supposed to* and forgot who I really was. When I got that Christmas pass from the hospital, I forgot where I was on my journey.

At that point in my life, I wasn't ready to do the whole recovery thing on my own. I was too raw. It was all too new. So even though I was *supposed to* be calm, I was totally freaking out.

So I asked my parents to drive me back to the hospital early. Instead of celebrating my favorite holiday, I went back to the eating disorders unit. The hospital was forty minutes away, and it was snowing heavily, but my parents drove me anyway. Because at that point, faced with the idea of spending all day around the indulgences associated with Christmas, I panicked. I retreated. I hid. Just as I had been hiding during my entire illness. I thought then that hiding was a weakness, but I know now that I just needed some extra help. I needed more time.

There was no Christmas tree on the eating disorders unit, only some lights strung along the windows. My family wasn't there, but other patients were, the ones too sick or too new to the program to go home for the holiday. We drew pictures and watched Christmas movies. We ate. We passed the time however we could.

Looking back now, the scene feels lonely. Back then, though, I was relieved. I was happy to spend the holiday season away from my family. I was ecstatic to escape the pressure of having to make choices about food. I wasn't ready to do that on my own yet.

It took me a long time to be fully ready to take care of myself, to truly realize, deep down, that I was worth nurturing and loving and accepting. It took two years in the hospital, off and on, in both partial and full hospitalization programs. It took two stays in residential treatment, each for three months, a year apart. It took medication and visits to therapists and nutritionists. It took relapses and almost ten years of *thinking* I was recovered but still having a lot more work to do.

I'm a work in progress. A messy work in progress that I've started over a thousand times. I've erased things and gone back to earlier sketches. I've stared at my painting so hard that the colors blurred before my eyes. I've been afraid to finish because it might not be perfect. Because there might be mistakes.

There *were* mistakes. I still make mistakes. But I kept going. I keep going. Because the life that I have right now—the worst day that I have right now—is so much more amazing than anything that came before.

As I mentioned, my disordered thoughts transformed into an eating disorder when I went away to college. College was a big change for me. I am *not* a big fan of change. I like to know what to expect. I like planning for things. And when things are good, I want them to stay that way.

I loved high school. I was good at school, and I loved being on the swim team. I fit in. Well, I *thought* I fit in. In reality, I fit in because I worked really, really hard at fitting in. Even with my friends, I was constantly aware of what I said and did.

Was I acting cool enough? Did I sound foolish? Was my shirt in style? Did my body look different from everyone else's?

I shouldn't have had to work that hard to feel good about myself, but it was all I'd ever known. I knew that when I excelled academically and was nice and perky and in a good mood, people liked me. So I always had to be in a good mood. I always had to be "on."

I decided to do the same thing in college. But I worried about what would happen if I presented my "best" self and these new people *still* didn't like me.

What then? My biggest fear was that I'd be rejected, that the gut-level, deep-down fears I had about myself (I was worthless, I was wrong, I wasn't as good as everyone else) would be proven true.

I knew they were true.

They had to be true.

Upon meeting my two roommates, I automatically compared my body with theirs and noticed that they were skinnier. I determined that this made them better and that I'd been right. I wasn't going to fit in.

So I decided to take things one step further. If I lost a little weight, everything would be okay. If I was skinnier, I'd be worthy. I started exercising. I started eating "better." My first morning at college, I woke up early and went to the gym across campus. Two girls in the dorm next door saw me leaving and invited me to go running with them.

Wow! I should have thought. *Friends! Just what I want!*

My mind didn't think that, though. My mind was so focused on losing weight to *get* friends that it rejected the fact that potential friends were standing right in front of me. Instead, my mind compelled me to say no and go to the gym instead.

They won't run long enough for me, I thought. *I need a better workout if I'm going to lose enough weight to fit in.*

I didn't become friends with those girls. I kept going to the gym. I ran instead of hanging out and watching TV. I ran instead of creating the bonding moments that cement friendships. I left classes early to work out and only ate what I thought I should. I had rules, and I followed them.

You might have rules, too. You might only eat certain foods at certain times. You might diet for a few days and then give up. You might binge on certain days of the week. You might have to wake up early to exercise for a certain number of minutes or do a certain number of crunches, even if your body is screaming for rest. You might know how hard it is to break these rules.

I couldn't break my rules. Not even when I realized I was miserable at school because I hadn't opened myself up enough to let myself fit in. Not when I transferred schools the next year and found that my eating disorder (because that's what it was, even though I hadn't realized or admitted it yet) had followed me. Not when I took a leave of absence from school to enter treatment once my parents found out what was going on.

I thought I'd been so careful. I thought I was hiding what I was doing. I thought everyone believed my lies. I said that I was eating healthier, that I just wanted to lose a little weight. I thought they didn't notice.

They noticed. My family noticed and my friends noticed. They saw me lying and saw me pulling away, saw me canceling plans because I was afraid food would be there.

I was afraid food would be *everywhere*. I was afraid that if I went to a party or opened up about how much I was struggling, how hungry I was and how I couldn't stop myself from restricting food and exercising, someone would take my eating disorder away from me.

The funny thing was that I actually *wanted* my eating disorder gone. I so wanted it gone. I was tired of pushing my body to its limit. I was tired of not sleeping because my bones hurt. I was tired of being hungry. I was tired of always thinking. Always measuring and counting and weighing.

I was tired of never feeling that I was good enough,

never feeling that I was getting closer to a finish line forever out of reach. I never lost enough weight. I never looked as good as I wanted to, as good as my friends and everyone on TV did.

I wanted to be happy.

But I couldn't stop.

One afternoon, I came home from my summer job. I was working at a law firm, answering the phone and typing memos and filing boring papers. I sat all day. I felt like a blob, so I needed—*needed*—to spend my lunch break exercising. I quickly changed into workout clothes, then hopped onto the bike in our basement. I'd have enough time to get in a mini workout before I had to go back, I promised myself. It would hold me over and hold back the anxiety until later.

And it did hold back the anxiety—until my father walked in twenty minutes later. I *never* stopped in the middle of a workout, but I stopped then. I stopped pedaling, sweat dripping down my face. I was busted.

I went into treatment after that. My parents made me go, but deep down I was glad. I was relieved. I knew I was sick. I hated my life the way it was. I hated it, but I couldn't stop myself from self-destructing. Not on my own.

Sometimes it felt as if I would die of anxiety if I didn't skip a meal, even though I knew I was getting sicker and sicker by the day. I needed to escape. I wanted to escape. I wanted to be free, like my friends were. The ones who could eat junk food at a sleepover. The ones who could skip a workout if they were tired and wouldn't freak out if they didn't know what restaurant people were going to more than a day in advance.

When I entered treatment, I was scared and relieved. Scared that the doctors would take away my eating disorder—the one thing that made me feel special—and relieved that they were going to make me eat. Make me rest. I wouldn't have to fight myself anymore.

I thought I was going to walk in the door and be cured.

I thought wrong.

The path to the other side

Treatment isn't a cure-all. This book won't be a cure-all, either, even though I wish it could be. Treatment *does* help, though. For me, treatment took the form of hospitalization, and it started me on my journey to recovery. It forced me to admit that I had a problem and gave me the coping mechanisms to use in situations that triggered my anxieties and obsession with my body. I learned methods to calm myself down and worked to unravel why I felt that I wasn't good enough for the world.

I learned about the messages my eating disorder sent me and how to distinguish them from my healthy voice. I went to groups on nutrition and body image, where we made sample meal plans and analyzed advertisements in magazines. I practiced speaking up to my family when they put too much pressure on me and telling my friends what I needed them to do to help my recovery.

I made lists of my goals and dreams, ones that I couldn't accomplish with an eating disorder. I started to remember what was good about me outside of my body.

And I ate. I ate regularly and fed my body so that it could trust me again. I fed my brain so that it started functioning properly. And as I ate, I saw that food didn't kill me. I saw that I didn't gain seven million pounds after eating one meal. That I could wear a different pants size and my friends would still like me. That even if the world told me I had to be a specific size, being—or trying to be—that size was killing me.

And if it didn't kill me, it would kill my spirit. It would kill what makes life worth living.

I learned all this—and then I left the hospital and relapsed.

Things came up in the outside world, situations that made me want to dive back into my eating disorder:

- Someone commented on my weight gain.
- A friend went on a diet.
- My parents kept staring at me while I ate.
- I wasn't invited to a party and felt left out.

I relapsed, and I wasn't able to pull myself out of the hole by myself. I got stuck again, so stuck that I needed more treatment. There are lots of types of treatment, but the right step for me was to go back to the hospital.

After I was discharged, I relapsed again. I repeated this cycle for a while, through various forms of treatment. Some people go through a similar process. Some people don't go to treatment but work toward recovery on their own instead. Some people relapse, while some recover on the "first try."

While the recovery process may vary, one truth is generally the same for everyone: It's hard to leave an eating disorder behind. It's hard to accept your body. So even though our experiences may differ, you may understand what I went through.

I left residential treatment the second time humbled. I had hit my rock bottom. I wanted a life. I wanted to go back to school. I wanted to be with my friends, who were having adventures without me. *They* had experiences and memories. *They* were living their lives.

My memories were of treatment and meal plans and body image homework. I wanted more. I wanted life, regardless of the weight I had to be in order to live it. I wanted myself back.

That's when things started changing.

There was still a part of me that wanted to be skinny.

There was still a part of me that felt like I wasn't enough. But I ignored those parts. I focused on what I wanted and what I needed to do to get there. I had goals and dreams. I wanted to get married and have kids. I wanted to be a writer. I wanted to go out with friends and laugh and swim and run without worrying about how many calories I was burning.

I wanted to eat my favorite foods. I wanted to sleep in without feeling like a sloth. (Sleep is good. My body likes sleep.) I wanted real life more than I wanted the fake life I was living in the fake body I had created.

I left residential treatment and followed my meal plan. I was honest about the times I didn't follow it, so I could get back on track. I gained weight. I freaked out about gaining weight. I freaked out for a long, long time.

But eventually I realized that I actually felt better when I wasn't so skinny. I had more energy. My sense of humor was back, and I laughed more. I wasn't cold all the time, and clothes fit me better. And as I ate and gained, I felt less anxious. Things leveled off. My weight stabilized.

It was a miracle! (Okay, not really. But to me, it felt like one.)

That wasn't the end of my recovery journey, though, because after a few years, I realized that I had more work to do. I had started internalizing society's messages again, started feeling like I wasn't good enough. I was exercising a bit more than I should and my eating became disordered. I wasn't doing anything awful or "sick," but I was on a quasi diet, not eating what I was really hungry for. I was trying to control myself, working hard to keep my body at the size that *I* wanted it to be, rather than the size that *it* wanted to be.

Bodies know these things. They have set points, where they're biologically supposed to be for maximum health and comfort.[1] Bodies are like machines. Not quite robot level, but pretty cool anyway. When you restrict your food, you feel hungry. Your metabolism slows down so your body can hold on to the calories you've already consumed. On the other hand, when you eat a lot, you might not feel hungry later.

Our bodies are amazing. And I needed to trust mine.

So I adjusted my actions and my mind again. I eased up on the exercise. I listened to my body. I let myself eat more because my body wanted more. I let my body find itself.

I let *me* find myself. I thought I was recovered, but I wasn't. Not all the way. I still had work to do. Sometimes, even now, I realize that I still have work to do. I'm human, and I exist in this very complicated world. I change. I adjust. I adapt.

I grow.

I'm not perfect. But I am recovered. For me, recovery

doesn't mean that I never get stressed out. Everyone gets stressed out; that's part of being human. But now, when I'm anxious, I know there are so many things out there that will calm me down more than restricting food or obsessing ever could.

When I compare myself with someone else, I try to identify what it is that I'm jealous of, then figure out how to fulfill that need in a way that doesn't make me feel awful. If I'm jealous that someone is prettier than I am, I don't necessarily yell at myself. I ask myself what "pretty" means. Do I want a new haircut? Do I need more sleep? Do I need to think about ways that I'm awesome, too?

Because I'm awesome. It took me a long time to realize that, but I finally do. My body is bigger now, and that's not a bad thing. Weight gain isn't bad. I am so much more than the wrapping paper around my heart, and so are you. We are a collection of talents and skills and pluck and drive and kindness. We can overcome obstacles and enjoy life.

When I was in treatment and expressing doubts about recovery, the counselors always told us about the importance of trust:

Trust in recovery and trust in my hunger.

Trust in what my body needs to function and thrive.

Trust that my coping skills work.

Trust that I'm a great person.

They told us to give recovery a try. To go all in. "If you eventually recover and don't like it, then you can always go back," they said. "You can go back to obsessing about your body. You can hide away from the world for the rest of your life. Just give recovery a try first. I promise you, you won't want to go back. Once you recover, you'll see. You'll never want to go back."

They were right. I never want to go back. Never.

You won't, either.

Recovery isn't magical. I still have bad body image days. I still feel guilty about not being good enough—not being a good enough writer, mother, friend, *whatever.* I still have hard moments in life—financial stressors and family stressors and so much more. But I *live*, regardless of these feelings and situations. I live and eat and move and make memories. I used the lessons that I learned in treatment until I internalized them. Until those beliefs of worthiness and enoughness became part of me.

You deserve to learn those lessons, too, whether you've been in treatment or are soon going to treatment or can't afford treatment. Whether you have slightly disordered eating or a diagnosable eating disorder. Whether you binge or purge or starve or overexercise. You deserve to know that whatever you've done, however you feel, you don't have to feel like that anymore.

In this book, you won't find any information about what

my lowest weight was or how many calories I ate. I don't talk about how long I exercised or what sizes I wore.

Those numbers don't matter. They don't matter because they didn't define me then and they don't define me now. But they also don't matter because you can be sick regardless of your weight. You can have a disordered relationship with food no matter how often you do certain actions. I don't want you to compare yourself with me or anyone else. I want you to focus on what's healthy for *you* and what is or isn't working in *your* life.

That's what matters. You matter.

This book won't cure you. No book can do that. You are the only one who can help yourself. And that's the amazing thing: You can help yourself. You can! You don't have to be thin to love yourself. You don't have to look or be a certain way. You can stop hurting yourself and hating yourself regardless of your size or your weight.

You can live regardless of your size or your weight.

You *are* enough.

My limitations

You may never be fixed. I may never be fixed.

Everyone in this world has something to work on, though. We all have things we can be better at. That doesn't mean we're broken. It doesn't mean we're hopeless cases.

It means that we're human, just like everybody else. I am not a perfect person, and I most likely did not write a perfect book.

I am writing this book as a straight, white female. I come from an upper-middle class background. I am cis, meaning that my gender matches the gender I was assigned at birth. I am married. I suffered from anorexia and excessive exercise.

I am privileged in many ways, and I did not and do not experience many of the things that readers of this book may experience. I am different from you. You are different from other readers, too.

In this book, I am not talking only to people with experiences like mine. This book is for *everyone* who suffers from disordered eating. This book is for all people who worry about their body and think that they are not enough.

Because of my limited background, I made it a point to research other experiences. I have talked to doctors, counselors, and nutritionists who work with various populations and varied eating disorders. I have talked with advocacy workers in the queer community.

I have interviewed people of color and men with eating disorders. I have spoken with transgender men and women, with people of varying sexual orientations, and with genderqueer individuals about their struggles with body image. I have spoken with individuals in the fat acceptance and Health at Every Size movements to discuss the importance of accepting your body size as it is and as it's meant to be.

It is my hope that regardless of your experience, you will be able to see your struggles mirrored in this book. You may not be able to relate to every chapter, and you may not identify with every piece of advice. But no matter who you are and which pieces of this book you relate to, your struggle matters. You are not alone.

That's the funny thing about eating disorders: When you're in the middle of your struggle, you think that you're the only person in the world who could ever feel this way. And, yes, portions of your experience *are* unique. You're the only one who has walked your path. But your emotions and fears are also universal. Lots of people think they don't matter. Lots of people don't feel at home in their bodies, whether they're unhappy with their weight or are dealing with a chronic illness.

Individual circumstances can make recovery more challenging, especially when eating disorders are misunderstood or overlooked.

Research into eating disorders in the queer population is still limited. However, the National Eating Disorders Association reports that as early as age twelve, "gay, lesbian, and bisexual teens may be at higher risk of binge-eating and purging than heterosexual peers."[2] Compared with other populations, gay men report more disordered eating behaviors such as laxative use, fasting, and purging.

Transgender people report more disordered eating than cis people, and they have to deal with more than one type of body image issue: both size and the conflict between their assigned gender and the gender they actually are. A 2015 study showed that 16 percent of transgender participants had been diagnosed with an eating disorder.[3] Yet this information is rarely heard in the mainstream.

The eating disorder stereotype is usually a skinny white girl "who wants to be pretty." But what about the boys who are struggling? What about nonbinary people and other queer people? What about people of color?

Some people develop eating disorders after they are diagnosed with a disease like diabetes, which demands an extreme focus on food.[4]

Fat people can have eating disorders.

Eating disorders do not discriminate based on body size, skin color, socioeconomic background, sexual orientation, health, ability, or gender.

We need to get familiar with the variety of people who have eating disorders so we can recognize symptoms in ourselves and in others. So we can stop making these distinctions and move toward becoming one community working together to erase eating disorders, remove barriers to eating disorder treatment, and get rid of factors that contribute to eating disorders, such as size-based discrimination and the pressure to adhere to societal expectations.

We all suffer, and we all struggle. We all feel out of place. But with that bond comes hope. With that connection comes the knowledge that you don't have to feel like this forever. Others have traveled this road and emerged into the sunlight. Others have healed.

Even if you don't connect to everything in this book, it is my hope that every chapter will add something important to the conversation about body image and self-esteem. That in the end, *you* will find hope and realize that every part of you is enough.

PART ONE

About Eating Disorders

CHAPTER 1
What Are Eating Disorders?

YOU MIGHT PICK up this book already knowing a lot about eating disorders. Or you might pick up this book knowing nothing about the specifics, nothing about the official words that doctors might throw at you. All you know is that something is wrong with your relationship with food.

You don't have to know all the lingo to get better, just as you don't have to be labeled a certain way to have a problem.

Eating disorders cover a wide variety of symptoms and arise because of a variety of factors, as I will discuss later. At their core, though, eating disorders are a collection of symptoms that interfere with your quality of life. If you have an eating disorder, you may worry about your body or about gaining weight or muscle. You may compare yourself to others. When you have anxiety or feel upset, you may find comfort in food—either by restricting it, purging it, or binge-ing on it. These behaviors (along with others) may soothe something inside of you that is hurting.

Some people with eating disorders don't eat enough and become malnourished and sick. Some people with eat-ing disorders eat too much, too quickly, and feel sick. Others eat and then throw up their food, and others are bothered by the textures of certain foods and are unable to eat them. Many people with eating disorders have complex rules about what foods are "safe" to eat and what foods are off-limits. Others might force themselves to exercise past the point of safety.

The criteria for diagnosis are complicated, but if you're able to go to a medical professional, you can be assessed and possibly given a diagnosis. But if you think something might be wrong with the way you eat or exercise, if you think that it may be out of control or disordered in any way, this book is for you. Whether or not you have an official diagno-sis from a doctor, whether or not you believe you're "sick" enough to have an eating disorder, and whether you're thin or fat, if you or someone in your life thinks your eating might be disordered and you think you might have problems with your body image, this book is for you.

When I was sick, I heard many people comment that

they would "love an eating disorder to lose weight." That's not how it works, though. Eating disorders aren't a diet. You can't simply borrow an eating disorder for a while and then return it when you're done. Eating disorders are hard to get rid of. They affect your brain like an addiction, and once you start receiving that sense of comfort from disordered behaviors, it becomes hard to stop these dangerous actions.

You *can* stop, though. If you are reading this book, there is a high chance that you are ready for a change. That you realize that whatever reassurance your eating disorder once provided you isn't worth the discomfort and lack of energy and sadness that now invade your days.

Maybe you're not quite ready to change *yet*, but you recognize that recovery *could* be a possibility someday. (Maybe.) There is nothing wrong with feeling like that. Recovery is a process, and the first step is recognizing that it *can* happen. You can read more about how to get there in this book.

Maybe your parent is concerned about how you're eating and bought you this book, but you haven't talked to a doctor or medical professional yet. Or maybe you've already been diagnosed with a specific eating disorder and are in the middle of treatment. You might worry about food a lot but believe it's not "serious" enough to be an official disorder. Maybe you know you can't afford treatment, so you picked this book up instead.

This book will not cure you, but it *can* start you on the road to recovery. It can educate you about symptoms that you have and situations that you encounter as you work to become healthier and to develop a happier, more accepting relationship with your body.

That relationship is possible.

I promise.

CHAPTER 2

What Types of Treatment Are Available?

DEPENDING ON YOUR eating disorder symptoms, your medical needs, your need for weight gain, your financial status, whether you have insurance, and even where you live, treatment options will vary. But you do have options—many options, ranging from attending therapy sessions to staying in a hospital.

If you have insurance, it may cover therapy sessions, psychiatrist appointments, and medication. Your insurance may cover hospital stays. Sadly, though, many insurance companies deny coverage for some eating disorder treatments.

That's why it's important to realize that if you can't get one specific type of treatment, you aren't doomed. Quite the opposite! There are so many different kinds of help you can get—support *is* out there, regardless of your family's finances or your life situation.

Though a lot of media about eating disorders focuses on hospitalization, that isn't the only option. You can seek out individual or family therapy if you and your doctor agree that it seems right for you. If you aren't sure where to begin, a school counselor might be able to direct you to resources for therapy or help.

I've included information at the end of this book about hotlines you can call and websites you can visit to seek out help that may be more affordable. There are free support groups, therapists who offer sessions on a sliding scale based on your ability to pay, and scholarship funds for eating disorder treatment.

Help is out there. Here are some of the main types.

Individual talk therapy

Therapists—who may be psychologists, counselors, or social workers—are medical professionals you can talk to. While all therapists will discuss your eating disorder symptoms in some way, they do have differences.

Some therapists will want to talk about your past in detail, to get a good idea of what led to your disordered eating. Therapists who practice psychodynamic therapy, a type of talk therapy, believe that as you talk about your past, you will come to see how it affects your current experiences, which will lead to self-knowledge and change.[5]

Other therapists will prefer to concentrate on what is going on now, on your behaviors and what leads to your actions. Cognitive behavioral therapy focuses on solving problems by concentrating on dysfunctional thoughts, emotions, and behaviors, then challenging those thoughts to change how you react.[6]

Therapists who use dialectical behavior therapy focus on painful emotions and behavior and teach skills to manage anxiety and negative thoughts.[7]

Mindfulness therapy, which was originally developed to use with depression, teaches how to deal with unwanted thoughts by accepting and becoming aware of them instead of immediately reacting and despairing.

If you have insurance, individual talk therapy is very likely covered, although you may be directed to certain providers in your network.

Psychiatrists

Psychiatrists are medical professionals who can write prescriptions for medications that may help manage anxiety, depression, mood disorders, and other mental health issues that may be contributing to your eating disorder or body image issues.

Family therapy

Family therapy usually occurs alongside individual therapy, often with a separate therapist altogether. Family therapy expands beyond talking about just *you* and your fears. Instead, it talks about the dynamic that exists around you and how the members of your family interact.

Medical care

An important part of treatment, medical doctors can check on you and watch for physical complications that might come up during your recovery.

Dietitians

Dietitians can help with meal plans and provide support to make sure that you're getting the right nutrition.

Support groups

Often led by a professional therapist or a recovered individual, support groups involve a number of people getting together to talk about issues with disordered eating. Some support groups have a specific focus (anorexia, bulimia, binge eating, males with eating disorders, queer people, adults), while others are open to the general population. All focus on recovery. Moderators will be aware of triggers, the topics or comments that might tempt someone to return to disordered eating. Some groups will include a meal or snack during the meeting.

Family-based treatment

In family-based treatment, also called the Maudsley approach, parents or guardians take an active role in helping their child recover through family meals. This type of treatment has proven very successful for kids and adolescents with supportive families.[8]

Outpatient care

In outpatient care you continue to live at home but attend support groups or appointments with nutritionists, doctors, therapists, or psychiatrists who are affiliated with a hospital or an eating disorder support organization.

Partial hospitalization

Partial hospitalization means you attend a hospital program for eating disorders, but still sleep at home. It is also called day treatment, since it usually runs from before breakfast until after dinner, most or all days of the week. Patients in day treatment still attend groups and meet with doctors in their program, but leave at the end of the day to practice coping skills at home.

Inpatient care

Inpatient care means you stay in a hospital overnight as well as during the day. It is often used for people with medical problems that accompany their eating disorder. As with partial hospitalization, there are group and personal therapy sessions and a strict schedule.

Residential care

Residential care is a long-term treatment where you live at a treatment center. It differs from inpatient care in that it is used for people who are medically stable. Therapists, counselors, and nutritionists are on staff, and the program works to ease you back into life with a lower level of care after discharge. These types of programs last anywhere from thirty to ninety days, sometimes longer, and are less likely to be covered by insurance, if you have it.

How to find a therapist

As you look for a therapist, it's important to know that all therapists aren't alike. Some may prefer cognitive behavioral therapy, while some may want to dive into your past. Some may use a tough-love approach, while some may be more forgiving and gentle.

Above all, though, it's important to find a therapist who has experience treating eating disorders. This way, you know that the person you are opening yourself up to won't respond with an insensitive comment. They won't talk about your weight above all else. They are educated about eating disorders and will help give you the tools to fight them.

Eating disorder therapists come from a variety of backgrounds and can be psychologists, social workers, or licensed therapists. The National Eating Disorders Association website has a treatment finder where you, along with your parents or guardians, can enter your location and which eating disorders you are struggling with, along with any other conditions you might have and what kind of treatment you desire—not just inpatient, but also individual therapy and family therapy. *Psychology Today*'s Therapist Finder and Zocdoc can connect patients to therapists in their area, as can some of the organizations listed in the back of the book.

Another step in finding a therapist is to have your

parents or caregivers contact your insurance company. In the best-case scenario, therapy will be covered. This may mean that you have to pay a small co-pay for each appointment, but the bulk of the costs will be paid by your insurance company. Sometimes, insurance companies will tell you that you have to pick from a certain pool of therapists in order for them to pay. A lot of insurance companies let you search for therapists on their websites based on specific criteria, and you can also check to see if a certain provider will be covered.

If therapy isn't covered, some therapists do work with patients on a sliding scale of costs to make things more affordable. That usually means that they set a price based on your family's ability to pay. (There's also a section in the back of this book about different scholarship funds that can help families pay for treatment.)

Also remember that you don't have to hire the first therapist you meet. This person is working to help you, and that's why it's important to make sure that you are a good fit for each other. Ask questions about what you will do in your sessions. How long has the therapist been treating eating disorders? What marks progress? Will you get homework? How will parents or caregivers be involved? What will your sessions be like?

This is *your* therapist, *your* treatment, and *your* life. You deserve someone who works well with you.

For queer people, it's important to find a therapist or doctor who understands specific issues you may be dealing with. It's fine to ask health-care professionals whether they're trained in working with queer people and are sensitive to their needs and experiences.

Alithia Skye Zamantakis, author of the article "My Journey to Eating Disorder Treatment as Neither a Man or Woman,"[9] talked to me about their struggle to find a therapist.

"They assumed that I was a man by my voice. Then they assumed I was a woman," said Zamantakis, whose pronouns are *they/them*. "It's hard to explain gender when you're dealing with so much else. It made me feel that treatment wouldn't even work."[10]

Zamantakis is now working with a therapist who doesn't specialize in eating disorders but who is queer and understands more about the trans community.

The cost of therapy can also be a barrier to many people seeking treatment.

Michelle, a biology student who has struggled with restrictive disorders, struggled with the cost of therapy. Even with insurance, she said that her office visits to a psychiatrist tended to be expensive. However, she has been in talk therapy for about a year and a half and has found a therapeutic outlet in writing and bullet journaling. "It's been especially helpful in tracking my emotions, mental health, and thoughts," she said.[11]

Stephanie Covington Armstrong, author of the memoir *Not All Black Girls Know How to Eat: A Story of Bulimia*, spoke about how the way that society viewed her made the search for help difficult.

"Because I am black, people, doctors, friends assumed that black women do not have eating disorders because we are all born with an innate confidence about our body," she said. "I wore a mask of confidence to hide my issues with food and low self-esteem from those around me. Falling outside of the strong black woman archetype was not an option so I fed into the narrative that I could cope with any and all trauma myself. It was taboo to seek mental health support in my community so I stuck to the status quo and suffered in silence, using food to quell the inner voices of doubt and shame until I could no longer hide and had to step outside of my comfort zone and seek help."

Though Armstrong didn't receive eating-disorder-specific treatment, she was able to find help.

"I joined a twelve-step program for my food problems and sought help with a therapist," she said. "I really believe that real recovery can only come by working threefold: body, mind, and spirit."[12]

Twelve-step programs are like a support group but are made up entirely of people dealing with an unhealthy behavior or addiction (rather than being moderated by professionals). They involve a process that includes admitting powerlessness over an addiction or problem, believing that a higher power can help, working with an experienced sponsor to recognize past errors and make amends, and learning to live according to a new, healthier set of behaviors.

As you progress through recovery, you will continue to reevaluate the type of care that you need. At some points, you may choose to change the type of treatment that you are receiving. Sometimes, you may need a higher level of care. At other times, you may be doing well and need less support.

Above all, it is important to choose the path to recovery that works for you and your individual situation. Because whatever that path is, help is out there.

PART TWO

Tools and Information
for Recovery

CHAPTER 3

Listening to Your Body

Why is eating so hard?

DISORDERED EATING IS often all about ignoring hunger cues. A lot of recovery is learning to recognize when your body is telling you to eat, and learning to listen and respect those hunger cues. Dietitians and nutritionists can help you get back on track. They can calculate (approximately, not exactly) how many calories you'll need per day to maintain or gain weight, based on your height, weight, frame, and activity level. They'll work with you to develop a meal plan that includes certain ratios of certain food groups. They'll tell you how important it is to drink water and how fats are amazing at keeping your skin smooth and your hair shiny.

Meal plans aren't an exact science, but a dietitian can work with you and adjust a meal plan to be just right. Every human body is different. Even if two people have the exact same height and weight, they'll still need different amounts of food to stay healthy. Everyone has different metabolisms. Everyone lives their lives in different ways.

Also—and this can be the hardest part to understand, accept, and embrace—their bodies are meant to settle in different places, based on their genetics.

I get it. It stinks. Maybe you want to weigh less than you do right now. You may work hard to achieve that goal. You may actually change your weight for a while.

But what's the cost?

I know I probably sound as if I'm lecturing you. Every body is different, blah blah blah.

Maybe I *am* lecturing you, though, in the sense that I'm imparting information. But information isn't a bad thing. Information is what our bodies are trying to communicate to us every single day. Every minute. Every second.

Can you tell when your body is tired? When it needs sleep or rest? Can you tell when your body is hungry? Thirsty? Full? Can you tell when your emotions are intense or your good judgment is clouded?

Some people can. Some people can't. Some people exist on a continuum between these two states, understanding their body's messages only sometimes. The rest of the time they have no idea what is going on in the slightest.

Either that or they ignore the messages completely.

Where do you lie?

What is intuitive eating?

In your recovery journey, you may hear about a concept called "intuitive eating," where the goal is to connect with your body's natural hunger and fullness cues. To eat when you are hungry and stop when you are full. To eat what you crave without judgment.[13]

Some people call this "normal" eating.

Here's the thing, though—I really hate the word *normal*. There *is* no "normal," especially when it comes to our society and food.

You may feel abnormal now because your relationship with food isn't the best. You may feel abnormal because you can't stop thinking about your body.

On the other hand, in today's world, aren't these disordered relationships and thoughts becoming more and more "normal"? Your mother may weigh herself every morning. Your best friends may skip lunch, and your brother may be on a diet to make weight for wrestling. When you turn on the TV or go to the movies, you don't see many plus-size actors and actresses. There are no fat Disney princesses. People go to the gym to "burn off Thanksgiving dinner" or run for hours to "earn that slice of birthday cake."

That's "normal" now, and it's all around us. So in a world where up is down and down is up and then down and then some other direction entirely, I think we should try to define our own "normal."

Society says that "normal" eating is organic foods, special diets, and "no carbs!"

Society says that "normal" eating is counting calories and trying to be small. Or trying to be toned and muscular. Society is loud.

Society yells so loudly that you can't hear yourself.

Society is wrong.

Here's what "normal" eating is, as defined in 1983 by dietitian Ellyn Satter, an authority on eating and feeding. The Ellyn Satter Institute counsels and trains both nutrition professionals and the public on how to eat with joy. Among its guidelines are eating when hungry and stopping when satisfied, eating foods you like, and considering nutrition while not restricting your diet. It emphasizes trusting your body and realizing that normal eating is flexible, rather than rigid.

I like this definition of "normal" way better than how many people define it. With this definition, you don't have to be a robot, making exactly sure that calories in equal calories out. Because let me tell you, trying to figure out exactly what your body wants is hard. Really hard. It's stressful and confusing and can really tap into the perfectionist streak that so many of us have.

What I like the most about Satter's definition is that food isn't only talked about in terms of energy and hunger. Food is discussed in terms of feelings, too. Because sometimes, when you're sad, a snack *may* make you feel better.

A snack isn't the *only* thing that could make you feel better, of course. Crying or talking to a friend or blaring music or writing in your journal or getting lost in a book or punching the air furiously while kickboxing might help, too.

Food is so many different things to so many different people.

Some people see food as something to consume to give them energy. Some people see food as a way to connect with loved ones.

Other people look at food as a way to classify themselves as superior to others, thinking that they're "healthier" because of their diet. They may see food as a way to judge themselves, and beat themselves up for having a snack.

But it's just a snack. Seriously. And if that snack is going to make you feel good in the moment after a hideous day, then have it and move on. Don't give it another thought.

That's the hard part, though. The "don't give it another thought" part. That's why you're reading this book. Because you *do* think about things like that. You think about things like that a lot. So did I, both when I was sick and when I was trying to recover and understand my body for the first time.

Recovery isn't easy. It's the hardest thing I've ever done. But it started with my body. It started with me listening to what my body needed *and* to what my body wanted. It started with me not being a robot, but being a human. One who makes mistakes and has too much food sometimes and too little food at other times.

We are all different. We have different homes and different friends. We have different family structures. Eventually, we'll have different careers and different lives. We don't all have the same foot size. We don't all have the same body size, either.

Your body will tell you what size it wants to be if you listen to it. Not all the time, not exactly, but most of the time.

For those in early recovery, intuitive eating is not recommended right away. It takes your body some time to heal from the damage you've inflicted. It takes time for it to trust you again. So at first, intuitive eating may be replaced by a meal plan set up by a nutritionist. It may be replaced by a certain number of meals and snacks per day.

But over time, your body will learn to trust you. You can choose to follow your stomach and your brain without worrying about how those choices will affect your body. You can do what you want. You can eat what you need.

EXERCISE: ARE YOU HUNGRY?

The next time you're hungry or full or tired, listen to the messages you start telling yourself (or start telling your body). Write them down.

Examples:

I just ate. I shouldn't be hungry.
I ate so much. I'm an awful person.
I'm tired, but I should go for a run.
Why am I so tired? I'm so lazy.

Are these things you're telling yourself true? These are all examples of what I call the "eating disorder voice," which we'll talk about in a later chapter. How is that voice making you feel? Why is it trying to make you ignore your body's signals?

CHAPTER 4

Nutrition: It's More Than Just Food Groups

What is healthy eating?

EVEN THOUGH IT'S important to listen to our body's signals, that's not an excuse to forget about good nutrition. And I know—believe me I know—disordered eaters will use any excuse to forget about good nutrition.

I'm not advocating for a life with perfect nutritional habits. Perfect nutritional habits are just another manifestation of an eating disorder, and for those struggling with orthorexia, the obsession with "clean" eating, a focus on ideal nutrition can do more harm than good.

"Clean" eating sounds like a good thing. It's the opposite of dirty, after all. And if being clean is good, that must mean that *we're* good, too. Right?

But "clean" eating is restrictive. It means analyzing

nutrition labels and obsessing about organic foods and additives. It's the opposite of balance.

As I was writing this book, I spoke with Lori Lieberman, a registered dietitian who specializes in eating disorders. Lieberman mentioned that one of the mistakes her clients make is trying to micromanage their food: "We think if a cupcake doesn't have nutrients like protein or fiber, then it's junk. But we don't have to get all of our nutrients from a single item. We don't eat single foods. Within the context of a healthy diet there is room for cupcakes."[14]

We don't have to eat "clean" all the time to get our nutrients. We don't have to eat all healthy foods all the time to fuel our bodies. Instead, we need to think big picture. Desserts can be part of a healthy diet, as long as our vitamin and food group needs are being met elsewhere.

We're allowed to eat processed foods, like store-bought desserts. We're allowed to eat fruits and vegetables, too. That's what I mean by good nutrition, and that's what balance is: a little of this and a little of that. Balance comes from strengthening and energizing your body with a variety of food groups while still allowing yourself to enjoy food and live a life that makes your taste buds dance.

(It is also pretty fun to imagine taste buds dancing.)

One of the first things all my treatment providers made me do when I was first diagnosed with an eating disorder was to give them a list of what I ate in a normal day.

I lied, of course. Partially because I was embarrassed of what they would think of me and partially because I knew that if I told them, they would make me eat more. And at that point, I didn't want to stop what I was doing. Not yet.

(I still made the real list of food I ate in my head, though. I still realized, deep down, that I wasn't eating enough. That I was hungry more often than not. That something was wrong.)

One thing that's pretty amazing is to watch a little kid eat. Kids get hungry. They whine and cry and ask for food. They ask for exactly what they want:

"Can I have a snack?"

"I'm still hungry."

"I'm done. I'm full."

Kids are incredible when it comes to listening to their bodies. To hearing and obeying their hunger cues. Kids leave a spoonful of food in the bowl because their bellies are starting to hurt. They eat an entire container of blueberries because they're delicious and they've been outside all morning.

Usually, kids eat three meals, along with two or three snacks. This is the schedule a nutritionist will probably put you on when you start recovery from an eating disorder. When I entered treatment, the meal schedule was extremely strict: breakfast, snack, lunch, snack, dinner, snack. It was the same thing every day, at the exact same time.

If you are currently in a treatment program or seeing a nutritionist, this is most likely the schedule you follow, too. In fact, Lieberman stressed how important it is *not* to try intuitive eating early in your recovery since all the chaos going on in your body and brain (such as eating disorder thoughts, anxiety, and suppressed hunger from slowed metabolic rate, for those who are restricting calories) will interfere with your body's signals. You may be so anxious that it will be hard to listen to your body. That's why meal plans—specific words on paper for you to follow—are so important.

Meal plans will change over time. In recovery, your metabolism (which controls how fast your body uses calories and how often you get hungry) is always shifting. But the plan's structure is important. That structure will remind your body that you are fueling it and that you will *continue* to fuel it.

Chronic illness and eating disorders

Chronic illnesses can also complicate a healthy relationship with food. Chronic illnesses are long-term or lifelong illnesses that can disrupt your life in many ways and that generally require a lot of time and energy to manage. Many chronic illnesses are incurable, and treatment may just be focused on managing symptoms, which can be a source of frustration, anger, and anxiety. Chronic illnesses are also often managed with strict diets, which can lead to a preoccupation with food and "health."

Examples of chronic illness include cancer, cystic fibrosis, chronic pain, Crohn's disease and ulcerative colitis, diabetes, celiac disease, migraines, and insomnia/narcolepsy, though there are many more.

People with certain chronic conditions also may have a hard time with body image and recovery. People with chronic illnesses like Crohn's, diabetes, or celiac disease may have to avoid certain foods, and many health-care practitioners may even suggest restrictive meal plans that are thought to help the symptoms of the chronic illness. The problem with these meal plans is that if people are already hyperconscious of their bodies, their eating habits, and their health, this focus on food can turn obsessive.

Sarah M. talked to me about her struggle to recover from an eating disorder after her diagnosis of type 2 diabetes: "I find that I'm even more obsessed with food sometimes because I'm trying to hit blood sugar goals and count calories, sugar, and carbs," she said.[15] Sarah said that because of her diabetes, she sometimes has to eat foods different from the ones she actually wants, which can interfere with the recovery goal of eating a variety of foods.

Some chronic gastrointestinal illnesses like Crohn's can make people lose weight when they're sick and gain weight when they're healthy. Strangers—or even loved ones—

may make comments about a person's weight or body changes, implying that they looked better when they were at a lower weight, even if that meant they were extremely sick. These comments can trigger unhealthy thoughts and assumptions in the minds of those already focused on their bodies.

Chronic illnesses don't only complicate and trigger eating disorders. Their symptoms might also *mask* eating disorders. Some people with eating disorders explain away their weight loss by blaming it on their physical disease. I spoke with one woman whose disordered eating was overlooked because others concentrated more on the physical symptoms that were going on at the same time: the stomach ulcer and acid reflux that made eating painful.

People with type 1 diabetes often lose weight before their disease is discovered.[16] After starting insulin treatment, though, the body can return to a higher, healthier weight. One person who was recently diagnosed with type 1 diabetes talked to me about the psychological difficulties that came with accepting this higher weight, especially after she had received compliments from others on her previous weight loss.

Type 1 diabetes is often diagnosed in adolescence, the same time that body image concerns start to take hold. It doesn't seem coincidental that girls with type 1 diabetes are

2.4 times more likely to develop an eating disorder than those without diabetes.[17]

Luckily, nutritionists take chronic illnesses, along with multiple other factors, into consideration when creating meal plans for people suffering from eating disorders.

Who are nutritionists?

Nutritionists are professionals who can create a meal plan based on your age, height, and level of activity. They can tell you how much to eat and the ideal eating times for you. They can tell you how much and what kind of activities you can do for exercise. If you're an athlete, your caloric needs will be higher because of your physical activity. The nutritionist will change your meal plan according to how your body reacts.

If you're seeing a nutritionist, you may hate your meal plan. You may want to disobey your nutritionist. A nutritionist may make a lot of suggestions that seem obvious, even annoying.

Of course, you know you need to eat healthy food in healthy amounts! *Obviously* you know all these things. You hate worrying so much about your body or food.

Knowing what to do isn't the same as doing it, though. That's what makes an eating disorder an eating disorder. Knowing the steps to take to recover isn't the same as actually taking them. That's why, if it's financially feasible, meeting with a professional nutritionist to talk things out can be helpful. It's one extra support on your journey, and that's never a bad thing.

Fat isn't bad

Many of us have been taught to think that being fat is a bad thing and that to be fat, or to become fat, is bad. Those messages are wrong.

As I mentioned earlier, fat is not bad. Saying that someone is fat is not a moral judgment. Fatness is not a sin. Fat is a term for describing bodies, like "tall" or "blond" or "freckled," and while the term should be neutral, it has become loaded and used as a weapon. "Fat" isn't the only term that has been weaponized to harm people; "obese" is a medical term that many people—including doctors and other health-care professionals—pull out when they want to justify discrimination against fat people.

A person can be fat and healthy. In fact, it can be much more dangerous to be thin than fat. A 2016 study of almost fifty thousand women and five thousand men age forty and older in the Canadian province of Manitoba showed that the skinniest women in the experimental group, those who were considered "underweight" or "normal weight," had a 44 percent higher risk of dying during the following seven years, while "overweight" participants had the best chance of survival.[18]

The Health at Every Size movement exists to show people that you can, in fact, be healthy at any size and that dieting actually doesn't work.[19] When you restrict your food, your brain thinks about eating more. Your metabolism changes so you need fewer calories to survive. Dieting makes you hungrier, which can lead to eating more than you're actually hungry for.

Your body is meant to stay within its unique size range. When you diet in order to break out of this range, your body will fight back. That's why it's so important for you *not* to push back at your body. Continuing to start and restart diets can actually cause health problems, and many of these illnesses are the ones attributed to the so-called "obesity epidemic"!

For example, in a 2016 Everyday Feminism article co-written with Melissa A. Fabello, professor, researcher, and *Health at Every Size* author Dr. Bacon noted that constant dieting can cause inflammation in the body. But then—surprise!—the effects of that inflammation (diabetes, heart disease, etc.) are blamed on "obesity."[20]

(I'll talk later about how the body mass index and the labels "overweight" and "obese" don't necessarily reveal anything about your *real* health.)

That's why it's important to figure out how your relationship with food really makes you feel and why it's so helpful to work with a professional. A nutritionist can help you eat more healthily. A nutritionist and meal plan can help your body *be* healthy and function the way it's supposed to, regardless of your size.

Sometimes getting healthier might involve gaining weight. Sometimes it might involve unintentionally losing weight as a result of being more active or learning to eat based on hunger cues. But here's the thing to keep in mind: Weight gain does not equal a failure. Weight loss does not equal a victory.

The true victory is finding the weight that is healthiest for you. It's different for everyone and can change at every stage of life. A healthy weight can mean being fat. And that's 100 percent okay.

You can retrain your body to eat regularly again

Before you can trust your body to know what it wants, you need to teach it how to eat regularly again. You need to reassure your body that you won't continue hurting it with your eating disorder. For so many of us, these behaviors are all our bodies know.

Our bodies are smart. When they're treated a certain way, they compensate. They fight back. Our bodies want to live. They want to protect us.

For example, if you give your body too little food, it will

slow down your metabolism. Your body will never know when it will be fed, so it will hang on to every calorie. Bodies want food because they're programmed for survival. Bodies will *tell* you that they want food.

But first you have to show your body that you're eating regularly again.

One of the main goals of a meal plan is to prove to your body that it *will* be getting food on a regular basis. To show your body that it can start to digest and metabolize food as it is supposed to. To communicate that it can trust you again. Because just as you may not trust your body to stabilize at a place where you "approve" of its shape and its weight, your body doesn't trust you, either. You don't have a history of taking care of it.

I certainly didn't take care of my body. Even when I decided to recover, I still didn't know what my body needed. I was used to being sick with my eating disorder. I was used to comparing nutrition labels. I was used to ignoring my needs. I needed help.

Lieberman said that she helps her clients recognize that they need a *range* of foods, not only to meet their nutrient needs, but also to satisfy. "Eating 'healthy' foods doesn't equal healthy eating," she told me. "You can eat lots of wholesome foods and not eat enough or still miss out on many nutrients. You need to allow yourself the pleasure of food, too."[21]

Refeeding syndrome and dealing with discomfort

If your body hurts, it may make you want to stop this whole recovery thing. This is especially true when you realize how physically uncomfortable it can be to start eating "normally" after you've stuffed or starved your body for so long. This physical discomfort *does* happen, although in varying degrees depending on your history of disordered eating.

I spoke with Dr. Mariela Podolski, the Medical Director of the Inpatient Unit of Walden Behavior Care in Rockville, Connecticut, who stressed the difference between an official condition called "refeeding syndrome" and the refeeding pains that many people experience in recovery.[22]

Refeeding pains refer to the discomfort that your body goes through as you start taking in more food on a regular schedule of eating. Because your eating patterns have been so erratic and disordered, you may be bloated and uncomfortable as you start eating more food. You may always feel full or even nauseous.

These are feelings that will pass, though. Your stomach and your gastrointestinal tract—a passage that goes from the mouth throughout your body—are not used to you taking care of your body and listening to your hunger pains. They need time to grow stronger and to adjust.

Dr. Podolski told me that the GI tract is a muscle, and likened the refeeding process to someone beginning a running program for the first time. After that first day of running, you might be sore the next morning. You will probably be sore the second and third day of running, too.

"Do you stop?" asked Dr. Podolski. "No. You'll be sore for a while, but as you keep training, your muscles get stronger and you're not sore anymore. Just like the muscles in your legs, your GI tract is a muscle, too, and you need to condition it to be stronger."

The way to do that is by continuing to eat and to push past the "soreness," in this case the bloating, the discomfort, and those feelings of fullness.

Refeeding syndrome is different, though, and Dr. Podolski stressed how dangerous this condition can be, along with how it is one of the major causes of death once a severely malnourished person (of any weight) starts eating regularly again.

When you starve yourself for a specific period of time, even for as little as five to ten days, according to Dr. Podolski, your body doesn't receive the nutrients that it needs from food. Since the nutrients aren't coming in, your body will pull from its reserves instead. Phosphorus is one of these important nutrients, and one of its roles is to manage and store energy in the body.

When you start eating again during the refeeding process, your body's needs shift. All of a sudden, it wants more and more phosphorus. But since you don't have any reserves left, your body's levels will drop.

And that is the dangerous part. That shock to your body is what causes refeeding syndrome, which can lead to heart failure, cardiac arrhythmia (abnormal heart rhythms), swelling, and even death.

Refeeding syndrome does not happen to everyone who starts eating again. But it can happen. And the more weight you lose, the more likely it is to happen.

Hypoglycemia, or low blood sugar, can also be a danger factor for those who have been restricting their intake. People who have been malnourished for a long time eventually get used to having low blood sugar. Even with incredibly low levels, they may say they feel "fine."

Except this means that there are no warning signs when blood sugar levels drop even more, which can lead to further medical complications and even death.

Eating disorders are scary, and not just while you're engaging in eating disordered behaviors. These behaviors can affect your recovery, too, and that's why it's so necessary to stop them now. Not later, but now, before you reach that danger zone.

That's why it's also so important to follow a meal plan under a nutritionist's and medical provider's care, especially if you are severely underweight or have lost a significant amount of weight. When dramatic changes happen to your body all at once, it can be dangerous.

Please don't let these side effects and potential complications scare you off. Staying sick is always worse than aiming for recovery, and the finishing line of recovery will outweigh any momentary uncomfortable and/or gross parts of the process (especially if you are appropriately monitored).

And recovery can be gross.

You may fart a lot. You may be constipated. Your stomach can cramp up and look so bloated you appear to be carrying a baby in there. You could burp a lot. You might feel full after half a sandwich because your stomach has shrunk so much. You may feel like you have to throw up.

Fun, huh?

Your refeeding pains won't last forever, though. As your body adjusts, the symptoms will ease and lessen. Your body will get used to working and metabolizing food the way it's supposed to. Your GI tract will strengthen. You will start to get hungry and full. You will start to recognize when you're hungry and full.

Little by little, and with the help of medical professionals, your body will begin to stabilize and trust you. You will learn to live—to eat—in a way that honors and satisfies your mind and your body, and that helps you be as healthy as you're able to be.

NOTE: If you don't have insurance and are worried about not being able to afford the medical care you need, there are treatment scholarships you can apply for, and some academic hospitals provide treatment to those willing to participate in a research trial. If you're underage, ask your parent or guardian to look into options in your area. If you *have* insurance but it denies you coverage, there's still hope: Many individuals and families whose insurance denies care end up petitioning their insurance company for coverage in these cases.

CHAPTER 5

Self-Esteem, or "What's Good About Me?"

How I struggled with self-esteem

WHEN I HAD an eating disorder, that eating disorder became part of my identity. It became what was good about me. I was good at losing weight. I could eat less than all my friends.

I was good at exercising. I thought I exercised better than anyone else. I was good at being skinny. People complimented me on my weight loss. People said they wanted to be like me.

It was the first time that anyone said they wanted to be like me.

When I was a kid, my brothers were good at sports. Really good. "Made two varsity teams as freshmen" good.

I was okay at swimming, but only made the B team.

I got stuck in the chorus when the school musical was cast.

I was good at school but was never the absolute best in my class.

I was good at reading, but you couldn't exactly say you wanted to be a reader someday.

Then I started losing weight.

It started off innocently enough. It was just a little diet. I learned all the rules to get in shape. I followed those rules. I exercised a certain amount and ate what I was "supposed" to. I lost weight. I started getting compliments.

I felt like a celebrity on the red carpet, with reporters and fans shouting words of praise at me, pushing to take pictures, wanting to be me and asking for my secrets.

For the first time, I *had* secrets. I had what I believed was a *talent*. For once in my life, I was good at something. I was the *best* at something, and I wasn't going to let anyone take that away from me.

For me, casting off this identity was one of the hardest parts of recovery. After years of starving and restricting, my eating disorder wasn't just a collection of behaviors anymore: It was who I was. Getting rid of that identity—stopping all related behaviors and letting go of the pride associated with being sick or "skinny"—is a difficult task, especially in a society where thinness is seen as a virtue.

For a long time, I didn't think I *was* good at anything else. I wasn't even good at *recovery* for a long time. I cheated on my meal plan and lied in therapy.

I tried to hang on to my eating disorder—my identity—

for as long as I could because it still made me feel special. I thought it was all that I had.

Why being thin couldn't be the good thing about me

After years of trying to hold on to my eating disorder, I couldn't do it anymore. I was too sad, too tired, and too hungry to keep doing everything that kept me sick. Losing weight got harder, too.

Despite what a lot of media says about weight loss, the more you try to lose weight, the harder it becomes. Many people don't realize that weight loss is not necessarily a matter of "calories in versus calories out." Studies have shown that people's hormones actually change after they go on restrictive diets. A 2016 study looking at the effects of television's *The Biggest Loser* found that the restrictive diets the contestants had been put on caused their metabolisms to slow down.[23] In fact, their metabolisms were still slow *six whole years* after they had left the show! Though they had lost weight over the course of the show, that weight loss wasn't permanent for most contestants, through no fault of their own. The act of weight loss made their bodies adjust, so their bodies needed less food to maintain their weight.

The body doesn't like being on a strict diet. The body

wants to stay within its own weight range. It fights back when you fight against it. That's what happened to me as my eating disorder continued. Losing weight became harder. I became more and more miserable.

Finally, I realized how much of my life I was missing out on. My friends were having fun and moving forward without me. I wanted what they had. I wanted to change. I wanted to recover.

So I started to do things a bit differently. I ate more. I listened to what my therapist said. I tried to sit with the discomfort that I was feeling.

The scale doesn't dictate your self-worth

I threw out my scale, too. This was a hard decision to make. For many people struggling with disordered eating, the scale feels like an important—even a vital—part of their life. At that point in my life, the scale felt like my friend. Seeing that number was something that I could count on. I didn't know what my life would look like if I couldn't have that stability every day.

Here's the thing, though: The scale *didn't* give me stability. In fact, the scale was more like a dictator than a friend. It told me what to do and how to feel based on the number that flashed on its display. It took away my peace of mind, my spontaneity, and my freedom.

Without the scale, I thought I'd feel lost.

But I also knew that without the scale, *I* could dictate my moods. *I* could decide whether or not I was sad or happy at a certain moment—not because of my weight but because of whatever else was going on in my life.

This simple action helped my recovery immensely. At first, it produced anxiety. I kept imagining awful things happening to my body. How would I know what to fix if I didn't have that number? But over time, not weighing myself got easier. I realized that I didn't necessarily have to fix *anything*, and the urge to step on the machine lessened. Because that's all the scale is—a machine. A machine that you don't *need* to own or use.

Sometimes, instead of throwing away their scales, some people hold scale-smashing parties, hitting it with a hammer until its insides are exposed as nothing more than metal parts. (This should not be done without adult supervision.) Some people decorate their scales and replace the numbers with affirmations.

Depending on who you live with, you may not be able to transform or get rid of your scale. Parents or caregivers might like to weigh themselves. They may resist your suggestion to throw it out. In this case, you can choose to avoid the scale. You can try to remember that you do not need the information it gives you.

That information says nothing about you as a person. It

says nothing about how you treat other people or what you enjoy doing.

It says nothing about how amazing you are, regardless of the size or shape of your body.

Why finding joy is so hard

"Enjoy life." It sounds so easy, doesn't it? Aren't humans wired to have fun?

Some people are, but some people are naturally more anxious. Some people are extroverts and love being around other people—while others are introverts and need quiet alone time to recharge.

Some people have life circumstances or a financial situation that makes it harder to have fun. Some may still encounter bullying or discrimination as they try to recover.

Even if you have a positive support network surrounding you, the early days of recovery will probably not involve you bouncing around the room and hanging out with your friends every day. Recovery is a long road. It takes a long time to find yourself. And a lot of that time will involve worry and fear.

I am a natural worrier. And for me, recovery led to way more anxiety at first. I was worried that I still thought about food. I was worried about my weight gain. I was worried that I didn't actually know what I liked. After all, I'd ignored everything but my body for years. I was so used to going through life with a one-track mind that it was almost impossible to think about what brought me joy. I didn't know what true joy was anymore or what I should want, both for my body and for my life.

How I found a way to feel happier

There's a saying that tells us to "enjoy the journey instead of focusing on the destination." If we're driving cross country, we'll miss out on all the gorgeous views out the window if we keep worrying about when we're going to get there. Life isn't just the end result; life is what comes between Point A and Point B.

You can look at fun the same way. You don't have to be awesome at something to enjoy it. You don't have to always do something just to win the gold medal or the blue ribbon. You can do it because it makes you smile or gets your mind off something you're worried about.

"Journey" activities are just as important as "destination" activities. And during my recovery, it was important that journey activities had nothing to do with my body, eating, or exercise. I had to learn to have fun outside of these areas of self-worth and "achievement."

At first, I could only think of two things I liked to do that didn't involve my body: read and watch TV.

Boring! I yelled at myself. *What kind of person has fun*

just reading and watching TV? Where's the excitement in that? Where's the struggle? Where's the glory?

I had to keep reminding myself that I wasn't striving for what I thought of as "glory" anymore. I didn't want "victory," or what my eating disorder had told me was victory. To my eating disorder, success was losing so much weight that I landed in the hospital. My disease wanted to hand me a gold medal as I was lying in a coffin.

Your disease wants that, too.

I don't want that for you, though. I want you to want more for yourself, too. I want you to stop entering races and racking up the blue ribbons. You don't have to be a professional all the time. You can be an amateur, too. You can have a hobby.

You don't always have to win.

I read a lot when I first started recovering. I watched TV a lot, too. I tried knitting and crocheting, but I got bored fast. I tried a lot of activities I thought I *should* like until I settled on ones I *did* like.

Here are some of the activities that truly brought me joy:

- Reading
- Watching TV
- Baking cookies
- Going to the beach
- Doing crossword puzzles
- Swimming
- Playing piano

The list was still short, and I still thought it was boring. I told myself that no one ever became special by going to the beach or doing crossword puzzles. And I wasn't all that great at piano. But I had to learn that I was special the way I was and that even the little things that brought me joy were important.

Even though I wasn't all that good at piano, playing and knowing I was improving made me feel happier than my eating disorder had. Even though these things were "minor," they made me feel good about myself.

You may have heard the phrase "you are not your body." If so, you probably roll your eyes and groan when you hear it. It's a cliché, but it's true, too. The people who love you, or who *will* love you, care because of who you are, not because of what you look like. They're not lying when they say that. There's no camera and film crew waiting to film your shock and horror as everyone shouts that this was all a huge trick.

You *aren't* your body. You *are* your smile and your interests and your passions. If you're passionate about television, watch television! Talk about your favorite shows with your friends! Join a fandom, draw fan art. Read and write fan fiction and go to cons. Dream up your own television show and write episodes!

If you like to swim, swim! You don't have to join a team or qualify for the Olympics. Feel your body glide through the water. Strap a pair of goggles on and do laps. Play Marco Polo with your friends on a hot summer day. Swim across a lake and have a picnic afterward.

If you like music, try an instrument! Play it even if you're bad, even if it takes you forever to learn the simplest song. You can listen to music. Sing at the top of your lungs in the car, even if you sound like a frog gargling water.

Find people who have the same interests as you and talk about them. Do things together. Being with other people is so much more fulfilling than being alone with your body. Especially when you spend all your time abusing and berating it. And if you want to be alone, embrace that, too. Solitude—when you're not spending the whole time unhappy with yourself—can be wonderful.

Once I started enjoying things, my life expanded. I became more than what my body looked like. I became Jen who loves reading stories with happily ever afters. I became Jen who likes country music. I became Jen who lives a life without always striving to be the best—and enjoys that life anyway.

In the process, I learned how to have fun. I learned how to love myself.

You can, too.

EXERCISE: FINDING CONTENTMENT AND JOY

Make a list of things that you enjoy doing. (These should be things *you* like doing. Not things that your *friends* like to do and not things your parent or guardian thinks you should do.) If the list is short, that's okay. Focus on one of these things and make an effort to do that activity sometime during the next week without focusing on achievement. How does this make you feel?

You can keep revisiting this list over time, as you think of new things you'd like to do and try.

EXERCISE: WHAT DO YOU WANT TO ACCOMPLISH AND LEARN?

Make a list of your accomplishments, knowledge, or talents that have nothing to do with your eating disorder, body, or how other people see you. Then make a list of other things you'd like to accomplish or learn.

CHAPTER 6

What Is Anxiety?

Anxiety and learning to trust your body

SOMETIMES TRUSTING YOUR body will make it easier to eat more food and stop when you are full. Sometimes thinking about your awesome qualities will help you stop comparing your body. But sometimes—lots of times—it's *hard* to trust your body. Maybe you just ate a huge meal and can't think of a single thing that's good about you. Maybe someone made a comment that your body looks different.

Maybe you don't feel comfortable in your own skin. Maybe you're anxious about something else in your life, like school, friends, or family. In fact, these nonfood-related anxieties can affect your mental health just as much as the fears that go along with food and your body.

One thing I heard over and over in treatment was that eating disorders are "not about food."

"Yeah, right," I answered. "Of *course* they're about food. Can't you see that I have a problem with eating?" What I didn't realize or admit, for way too long, was that these professionals were right. My problems *weren't* just about food.

Food is food. Food is fuel. Food should be neutral. It was my fears about being accepted and being "perfect" that were causing that anxiety.

Anxieties can feed into other anxieties. If you're nervous about money or parent problems, if you're being bullied or having trouble in school, you may use eating disorder behaviors to distract yourself from what's really going on.

You may also be genetically wired to be anxious. For many, there is no "logical" reason to feel so on edge. Yet they are. And these feelings are just as valid.

So what do you do when you start feeling anxious? When someone says that you look "healthier," do you automatically translate that to "you look fat"? Do you get angry at your body for being a different size and shape from what you want it to be? Do you do something that will hurt you in the long run? Anxiety is awful. When I get anxious, I feel it throughout my body. My chest tightens, and my muscles tense. My heart beats faster, and my breath comes more quickly. Every inch of my skin feels alive and constricting.

Everyone manifests anxiety in different ways. Some

people perspire. Some people have full-blown panic attacks, which can feel more like heart attacks. Symptoms of a panic attack include feelings of fear or danger, dizziness, shortness of breath, heart palpitations, weakness, numbness or tingling, hot or cold flashes, sweating, and chest pressure.[24] Some people take medication to ease their anxiety symptoms. Some do deep breathing or yoga or wait it out.

Some don't know how to deal at all and cope by hurting themselves instead.

Fight, flight, or freeze, and why we feel anxiety

We can panic when we encounter a situation that is unknown to us because the unknown can feel like a threat. In a situation like this, we have three options: fight, flight, or freeze.[25]

Animals have similar reactions when they are faced with threats to their survival. Their sympathetic nervous system releases hormones that get them ready for action.[26] When animals are threatened, they are instantly alert. The process is automatic and subconscious to ensure survival—without a thought, animals are ready to fight or flee.

Human beings are animals, too, and while we might not face the same threats as mountain lions in the wild, our bodies work in similar ways. When we face a threat, our bodies react. Our heart rate may pick up. We may get pale or flushed. Our blood vessels and pupils dilate, and our body shakes. Digestion may be affected.

We're not mountain lions, though. Our daily anxieties aren't the same as those of animals fighting for their lives in the wild. Our worst-case scenario usually isn't death.

It can feel just as dire, though, especially for those with eating disorders or low self-esteem. When someone calls you a name and your heart starts beating faster, it can feel as if you really might die. You may want to run away.

A lot of times, your way of escaping this feeling will be to do exactly what your eating disorder wants you to do. Your eating disorder is a coping mechanism, a way of soothing and distracting yourself from the real problem. These obsessions and harmful behaviors are your disorder's version of "fight or flight."

In the short term, falling back on your eating disorder might make your anxiety feel easier to cope with. But then what? What happens after, when you still haven't dealt with the initial threat, issue, or encounter that hurt you? What happens the next time you face the problem and you still don't know how to solve it?

You'll be even more tempted to turn to your eating disorder again and again.

That's how the cycle continues. That's how people get sick and stay sick. Anxiety feeds off itself. The more you indulge it and turn to harmful coping mechanisms, the stronger it returns. You need to *face* anxiety—to *tolerate* anxiety—to learn how to deal with it and gradually lessen its place in your life.

That's the hard part. That's the awful part. But there are techniques that can help.

The diversity of people's brains and eating disorders

Most people experience anxiety at one time or another, but some people also deal with anxiety or challenges that are related to other specific conditions.

Though much of society is set up for people whose brains work in one particular way, there's huge variety in the ways brains work. That variety is called "neurodiversity."

"Neurotypical" describes anyone whose mind works in the way that society is set up for.

"Neurodivergent" or "non-neurotypical" describes anyone whose mind differs from the type the world is set up for. For example, autistic people, people with some mental illnesses, and people with attention deficit hyperactivity disorder (ADHD) or dyslexia are generally considered neurodivergent.[27]

What does this look like in daily life? For example, the loud noise of an automatic hand dryer might not bother a neurotypical person, but to someone who's bothered by unexpected loud noises, like many autistic people, that sound can be unbearable.

When it comes to eating disorders, neurodivergent people face their own unique set of challenges, particularly because they might already face challenges with a world that isn't set up to accommodate them.

One type of neurodivergence is autism spectrum disorder, where people have difficulty with social skills, sensory processing, speech, and nonverbal communication, among other things.[28]

I spoke to writer Rachel Simon, who is on the spectrum and was diagnosed as anorexic with avoidant restrictive food intake disorder tendencies.[29] This diagnosis often overlaps with autism, as both disorders can involve a sensitivity to the texture and smell of certain foods. For Simon, her eating disorder wasn't so much a desire to lose weight, but a lack of desire to eat. Eating was a chore. She didn't care. Often, eating certain foods disgusted her.

Katie Linden, a mental health counselor who was diagnosed as autistic when she was thirty-one, told me how her eating disorder started as a result of accidentally skipping breakfast one morning because she was late for school.

"By lunchtime, I had discovered that being hungry made all of my anxiety disappear—I felt kind of numb and floaty, and I was distracted from the abuse and isolation going on around me. After that, I started trying to restrict so I could feel like that all of the time."[30]

It wasn't until Linden's diagnosis years later that she realized that much of her rigidity, anxiety, and obsession with detail had to do with being autistic, not just having an eating disorder.

Intense, excessive feelings of anxiety that don't go away can be their own disorder, though, and can exacerbate an eating disorder.

There are many different types of anxiety disorders, but all involve a persistent, serious feeling of worry and fear. This isn't a basic, occasional feeling of nervousness or uncertainty over a test. This feeling is not temporary and often gets worse over time. Anxiety disorders stop people from living their lives and affect their behavior in school or with friends.

Anxiety disorders can include panic attacks, which are different for everyone, but often involve a combination of physical symptoms (racing heart, nausea, churning stomach, sweating) and snowballing thoughts (*I'm having a heart attack; this is never going to end; am I dying?*).

Some anxiety disorders, like generalized anxiety disorder, involve anxiety extending to various aspects of your life.[31] Others, like social anxiety disorder, can be focused on specific situations, like speaking in public, meeting new people, or returning to a specific place or circumstance in which you previously suffered embarrassment.[32]

What to keep in mind about all anxiety disorders is that they:

1. are not your fault,
2. interfere with your life,
3. can make anxiety around food worse.

Obsessive-compulsive disorder is an anxiety disorder where the sufferer has both obsessions (repeated thoughts or images that cause anxiety) and compulsions (an urge to repeat a behavior to relieve the anxiety).[33]

Common obsessions include fear of germs, fear of death, fear of being violent, and the need for things to be perfectly neat and symmetrical.

Common compulsions include washing hands, arranging and ordering things, excessive cleaning or counting, and checking to make sure things are a certain way.

However, obsessions and compulsions are different in everyone. People with OCD can also have intrusive thoughts, which are scary or disturbing and come up automatically.

I myself have been diagnosed with obsessive-compulsive disorder, which was a huge factor in my anorexia. With OCD, the mind fixates on something, and the nervous system believes danger is imminent if the person doesn't complete a certain action. For me, I had to eat a certain way and exercise a certain number of minutes. If I didn't, I would feel that sense of anxiety and impending doom. The only way I could relieve it was to perform that compulsion.

Anxiety is just one of the many mental health conditions that can exist alongside an eating disorder.

People with post-traumatic stress disorder can have eating disorders. PTSD is a condition of extreme stress or anxiety following a traumatic event or the threat of a traumatic event.[34] While often talked about in terms of soldiers returning from war, PTSD can affect anyone who lives through an awful event. In fact, the event only had to seem traumatic to the sufferer to cause post-traumatic stress.

PTSD symptoms can include flashbacks, bad dreams, scary thoughts, and self-blame. People may avoid situations that trigger their stress response, which can include physical symptoms like sweating or a racing heartbeat.

Some people with eating disorders also have mood disorders such as depression or bipolar disorder.

Depression isn't just being sad or moping around. It's not just canceling plans because you're not in the mood. Depression affects your whole life. Its severity varies, but depression can cause irritability, decreased energy, feelings of guilt, feelings of unworthiness, a sad or anxious mood, appetite changes, changes in sleep patterns, and thoughts of death or suicide.[35]

Depression makes it hard to gain the motivation to recover from an eating disorder. In short, depression can make you hate yourself. Add that to the way malnutrition affects your brain, and recovery becomes even more difficult.

People with bipolar disorder suffer periods of depression interspersed with periods of elation, or mania.[36]

During manic periods, people with bipolar disorder may have a lot of energy or feel very jumpy, even irritable. They may believe they can do many things at once and take on lots of responsibilities. They can have trouble sleeping and do risky, dangerous things.

Depressive periods are the crash after all this energy. During a depressive episode, people with bipolar disorder can be sad and hopeless, have low energy, and feel worried about everything.

A 2011 study found that 14 percent of people with bipolar disorder also have an eating disorder.[37]

The good news is that therapists are trained to recognize these co-occurring conditions. They can help you understand how your eating disorder and any other disorders interact and what you can do to be the healthiest version of yourself you can be. Psychiatrists are also trained to understand how medication for various conditions affect your body and your brain.

Anxiety makes life seem a whole lot harder. But it is manageable.

There is help.

EXERCISE: WHAT MAKES YOU ANXIOUS?

Take some time to think about instances when you feel anxious. What types of events or activities make you feel that way? How often does it happen? What do you think you can do to make those situations easier to deal with or get through?

CHAPTER 7

Tool Kit of Distress Tolerance Skills to Help with Anxiety

Types of anxiety and techniques that can help

DISTRESS TOLERANCE IS one of the skills taught in most eating disorder recovery programs, and it can help you deal with anxiety.[38] Distress tolerance is the idea that by facing anxiety, you will learn—and you will teach your body—that anxiety can't get the best of you. That you can push through it. That you don't have to be overwhelmed by the signals your body is flooded with. If you simply wait out the anxiety and distract yourself, you'll prove there never was a threat to begin with.

Of course, many people do have problems that are legitimate threats. If you are faced with abuse or are afraid you're in danger, please talk to someone you trust. These situations *should* be sources of anxiety, and your feelings are prompting you to act and to reach out.

Distress tolerance isn't for legitimately dangerous situations. But what about anxieties about eating breakfast? Is eating breakfast a real threat? Does it make sense to fear eating breakfast so much that you turn to your eating disorder or start thinking terrible things about yourself?

What if you're anxious about going out with friends? If you panic about going out to dinner or to a birthday party, might it be because you don't want to eat in front of other people? Are you afraid you'll eat too much in front of them and lose control? If not, what do you think is causing your anxiety?

Even if you know you "shouldn't" be nervous in these situations, you may be. And that's okay. That's what distress tolerance will help you address.

Whatever the situation, you may be anxious and distressed. So how can you get rid of these feelings while not acting in ways that are harmful or that continue this cycle of anxiety?

You ride the wave. Researchers have set forth a theory that anxiety is like a wave: In every situation, your anxiety will start off low, rise and build to a crest, and then gradually fall once again.[39]

When you are nervous or afraid, it is important to remember that these feelings won't last forever, even if it feels as if they will. Your body cannot sustain this "fight, flight, or freeze" response forever, especially once it realizes that you aren't really going to die.

Things will calm down. You just have to distract yourself in the meantime, while your body surfs the wave. You want to get through the moment until the pain and fear pass. Instead of listening to your eating disorder, which may reduce your anxiety but will hurt you in the long run, you can use distress tolerance tools instead.

Instead of using an unhealthy coping mechanism like disordered eating or exercise, you can distract yourself. You can talk to a friend, or use the specific coping skills that I discuss in this chapter.

After a while of continuously using your new coping skills, the wave of anxiety won't crest as high. Riding the wave won't take as long. You'll have experience pushing back against your eating disorder urges so you won't be tempted to use them anymore.

That's how you reach recovery. That's how you calm the waves. But you'll never get there unless you first try to surf.

Distress tolerance tools are highly personal. What works for one person may not work for another. But if you can distract and soothe yourself until the pain passes, you will get through the moment without making things worse.

When you're anxious, it's hard to concentrate on anything else. You may be thinking about your body, eating or not eating, or what people think of you. You don't have the time or the brain space to worry about how to stop yourself from worrying because you're too busy already worrying!

That's why distress tolerance skills come with a bunch of handy-dandy acronyms and abbreviations so you can remember how to help yourself in the moment. Keep reminders of these tools nearby so that when you need help, you don't have to think too much. Try writing some of these techniques down on an index card and keeping it in your pocket, or if you have a phone, use it to take pictures of these pages. That way, when you need it, help will be right there.

You can pick and choose, too. You can try the skills that you know work best for you or you can try them all. You can also create your own ways of getting through your anxiety. It's important to remember that everything is individual and that you shouldn't feel constrained by the tips here.

Distract

First of all, you can distract yourself. What kind of hobby or activity can you do that occupies a lot of your mind, and maybe even your body?

I used to play piano when I had urges to exercise. Moving my fingers across the keys helped pass the time until my anxiety wave crested and started to fall.

Lots of the people I met in treatment centers knit or crocheted. You may like to color or draw, watch TV or movies, listen to music, play games, talk to a friend, or use fidget toys (like fidget spinners, kinetic sand, spinner rings, or Rubik's Cubes).

The goal is to choose something that can occupy your attention for an extended period of time, so anything goes!

Make a list of pros and cons

When trying to convince yourself not to use a harmful coping mechanism, weigh the pros (good things) and cons (bad things) about the situation. Ask yourself what would happen if you acted on what you're tempted to do. How would this bring yourself toward your goal of self-acceptance? What would happen if you sat with the anxiety instead?

A list of pros and cons will help you use logic instead of immediately turning to your harmful coping mechanism.

IMPROVE the moment

When you feel anxiety, you know that riding this wave is going to be hard. It's going to be painful, and it will feel as if it's lasting forever. That's when you need to think about how to make the ride better. How can you IMPROVE the moment?

Here's our first fun acronym of the book!

I—Imagery

You know how looking at art can relax you? Or how you might feel more at peace when you see a painting of a beach scene or those cute baby animals? Maybe you love pictures of old crumbling castles or lighthouses, or even those modern paintings with bright shapes and colors splashed across a canvas. When you're stressed, try to see one of those pictures in your mind. Paint a mental picture of whatever relaxes you. Escape into that image to forget about your anxiety.

M—Meaning

If you can find meaning in your situation, it can be easier to bear. Obviously, having an eating disorder is awful. Obviously, being worried about your body all the time isn't what you want. You might be dealing with some other stressful things, too. But is there any positive outcome that could result from your being in this situation? Maybe you'll eventually find your calling helping others. Or you'll prove to yourself how strong you can be when you overcome this hurdle. Try to put yourself a few months or a year in the future, then look back at yourself now and lend some words of hope about how wonderful life will be someday.

P—Prayer

If you're religious or believe in a higher power, you can pray for strength or guidance. Whatever prayer means to you—

and prayer can take the form of many things—you can call upon it to get you through a stressful situation.

R—Relaxation

Relaxation is a way to ease the stress you feel when you're worried. It often involves focusing on your body to see what areas are tight and tense, often with deep breathing. Many people relax through yoga or some gentle stretching. You can even get a massage, if that's comfortable and affordable for you. Often if your body is calm, your mind will follow. I'll talk about relaxation in more depth in Chapter Ten.

O—One Thing at a Time

The situation you're in right now may be awful. You may think that you will never feel better and that there's no point in trying.

This is where you need to remember that these single moments of rejecting bad coping mechanisms *do* matter. They build upon each other like links in a chain. And once those links add up, that chain will be strong enough to lock up your eating disorder and send it away for good.

This can only happen if you don't despair, though. Take each situation one at a time and moment by moment. Don't think about the past or the future or how you might feel tomorrow. Think about how you feel *now* and how to push through *that moment alone*.

V—Vacation

I *wish* I could tell you to book a flight and go to Hawaii. It would be pretty amazing to do that whenever I was stressed. "Doctor's orders, everyone!" I'd exclaim, then I'd jump on a plane and spend a week at the beach.

Unfortunately, we all can't afford vacations. We *can* take vacations in our mind, though. Your imagination can take you anywhere you want to go.

Close your eyes for a minute and picture yourself somewhere relaxing. It might be a beach at sunset. It might be in courtside seats at a basketball game or riding a bike through a forest.

You can also take a literal vacation, even if you don't travel across the world. Take a walk to the park down the street. Call a friend and talk about your favorite TV show. Give your mind a vacation from what you're worried about.

E—Encouragement

You might not be a cheerleader with pom-poms and the ability to do a cartwheel, but you can cheer for yourself. Give yourself a pep talk and remind yourself of all the challenges you've overcome before. You've been fighting to get better, and you're doing a great job. Tell yourself what a warrior you are and can be. This evidence can be your armor in this battle, too.

Wise mind ACCEPTS

Deep down, you know that hurting yourself isn't the answer. You haven't done anything to deserve the agony of your disordered eating or overexercising, or all the hurtful things you might say to yourself. You know there's another way to live your life. You know what you have to do. You just don't really want to do it yet. Or you can't make yourself do it.

Please keep trying.

Researchers have coined the acronym ACCEPTS to describe activities to bring yourself back to this wise mind. Some of them may sound silly and simplistic, things a little kid might do for a project. But you're not aiming for sophistication here. All you want to do is ride the wave. Let these activities be your surfboard.

A—Activity

Find an activity to distract yourself from the anxiety, one that gives you joy. It can be anything. Painting or coloring. Knitting. Reading comic books or playing a role-playing game. Writing a poem or watching cartoons. Anything! (Anything safe that won't trigger any of your eating disorder behaviors, that is.)

C—Contributing

Do something to contribute to the world and focus your brain on someone else. Make a card for someone you care about.

Volunteer. Pack up a bunch of books you don't read and send them to a shelter or a classroom that needs them. Get involved in politics. March for a cause.

C—Comparison

If you compare yourself with other people, usually you compare yourself with someone "better," right? The goal here is to do the opposite—instead of thinking about what you *don't* have, think about what you do have. Think about what you can be grateful for and what makes you different and valuable.

E—Emotions

Try to push away your main emotion of fear or anxiety by using a positive, opposite emotion instead. If you're sad, listen to happy music. If you can't stop crying, read a silly book. Ask a friend to tell you a funny story or go see a light-hearted movie.

P—Pushing Away

Simply tell yourself that you won't deal with these negative thoughts and urges right now. When you have a thought that gives you anxiety, picture a stop sign in your head. When you think bad things about yourself, tell yourself those thoughts aren't helpful.

T—Thoughts

Distract yourself with other thoughts. Count as high as you can. Do a crossword puzzle. Think of all the prime numbers. Try to find every color of the rainbow in the room that you're in, or an item that begins with each letter of the alphabet. Occupy your mind so your harmful urges can't get through.

S—Sensations

Engage in an experience where your body is distracted from what's going on around you. Smell a favorite scented body lotion or take a walk in a garden. I love the smell of bookstores, while others may love listening to loud music. You could take a hot shower. A cold shower, even—that's definitely shocking! You don't want to hurt yourself; rather, you want to engage your senses in a therapeutic manner.

Self-soothe

In this category, therapists and professionals focus on using the five senses (taste, smell, sight, hearing, and touch) to distract yourself from your anxiety. The goal is to focus on your body in a gentle way, one that helps you realize that your body is enough as it is and that it deserves relaxation and joy.

When I was sick with my eating disorder, I created a self-soothing "tool kit." This was an actual box that contained items to help me relax and distract myself, along with reminders of additional coping skills I could use. When I got an urge to use my eating disorder, I would open up my little box and use a few of these self-soothing objects.

Here are a few options, although individual choices will vary tremendously:

Taste
Tea or hot chocolate. A food associated with a positive memory. (Make sure not to choose a food that might trigger an eating disorder behavior.)

Smell
Candles or scented lotion.

Sight
Pictures of people you love. Note cards with positive sayings on them or cards from others expressing their belief in you. Photos of places you want to visit one day or things you want to do. Art supplies.

Hearing
Your favorite songs. A white-noise app. The sounds of nature. Something funny on television.

Touch
Play dough. A fidget toy or stress ball. Lotion. Nail polish.

At first, distress tolerance will be difficult. You might still feel anxious. Your brain might be loud, and your body may twitch. You could be tempted to do something that you know would be wrong. These urges will still be there, but over time and through practice, your brain will get quieter. You'll get better and better at riding the wave.

You may always have anxiety, and there's nothing wrong with that. Anxiety is part of the human condition. Now you have tools, though. Now you can take action.

EXERCISE: MAKE YOUR OWN SELF-SOOTHING TOOL KIT

What items do you want to include in your self-soothing tool kit? Use this tool kit the next time you feel stressed or want to engage in eating disorder behaviors and bad coping mechanisms.

CHAPTER 8

Assertiveness, or "Use Your Voice"

Trying to feel confident

THERE ARE PEOPLE out there who seem born with confidence. One of my friends is like this. From the time we were in elementary school, she never cared what people thought about her. When they insulted her haircut, she laughed. She ate dessert without a second thought. She broke up with guys and was broken up *with* and then moved on, still assured of her self-worth.

This friend was a foreign creature to me, as strange as a little green alien with two silver antennae. I didn't understand how she functioned. I didn't understand how her mind worked, just as she couldn't understand mine.

Why *didn't* I like myself?

Why *couldn't* I speak up for what I wanted?

And why wouldn't I let myself eat that dessert—it looked so delicious!

My friend and I needed a translator to get through to each other, and my work in recovery was that translator. It took me a long time to realize that it was possible for me to feel that same sense of belonging in my life, too.

When I had an eating disorder, I didn't like myself. I didn't think my voice was worth anything. You may feel the same way. You may feel as if you don't belong in your body, whether it's because of your size or your gender or something else. You may feel wrong. Faulty. Not "enough."

I didn't think I was "enough" to be an active participant in the world, to step forward and proclaim: "This is who I am!" I thought I'd be laughed at. I thought people would judge me and call me boring. A loser. Pretentious.

I was so afraid of judgment that I wouldn't let myself live. I wouldn't let myself take risks because I was afraid of rejection. I wouldn't reach out to make new friends because I was scared they wouldn't like me.

So instead of living, I turned inward. I thought about my body and weighed myself a lot. I got angry at my body for growing and developing the way bodies are *supposed* to when they go through puberty, when we're not trying to actively control them. I thought I didn't deserve to speak up, so I didn't.

You might dislike yourself now, but you are special and deserve a voice

You may feel the exact same way I did. You may think that you're defective, that you need to hide behind a veil of disordered eating. Or you may hide behind a persona you've created, one that's harder to maintain every day.

You may not like who you are, but the combination of qualities that make you *you* are so important.

You *can't* be someone else, and you deserve to live and to be, just as you are. You deserve to ask for what you want. Part of embracing yourself will be to start using your voice, challenging your thoughts, tolerating anxiety, and putting yourself out there.

Once I realized that it was okay to be me, it became easier to take risks. I raised my hand in class more because if I gave the wrong answer, well, who cared? Yeah, I wouldn't be right, but in the end, was that so bad? The teacher would say no, and she'd call on another kid. Maybe that kid would be wrong, too.

Learning to speak up to friends and family

Strangely, the hardest shift for me was learning how to be assertive with my friends and family, the people who were supposed to love me unconditionally but who often expected me to be soft-spoken and agreeable, to not speak up when I was angry. I realize that in this instance, I'm lucky. My family *does* love me, even if my parents criticize things I do occasionally. My friends *do* respect me, and the ones who didn't, I eventually removed from my life.

Some of you may not have such support systems around you. Your parents may work so much you never see them. Your classmates might make fun of you. Your best friends might be too far away to give you a hug when you need one.

Assertiveness is hard when you're met with rejection or with people who don't care.

It's still worth speaking up, though. You're still worth it. You deserve to ask for what you want and what you need.

IMPORTANT NOTE: If you're in a situation where you fear violence if you speak up for yourself, please speak to an adult you trust or seek professional help from a therapist or support group. Resources at the end of this book can help you connect with professionals.

EXERCISE: WHAT ARE YOU AFRAID OF?

Make a list of things you have been afraid to ask for or speak up about. These could be actions you need people to take, comments you want people to stop making, or an issue that you feel strongly about.

Why haven't you been speaking your mind? What's the worst that could happen if you do?

CHAPTER 9

Cognitive Reframing, or How to Change Your Thoughts

How cognitive behavioral therapy can help

HAVE YOU EVER told yourself that you aren't good enough: not smart enough, not thin enough, not nice enough, or not "enough" in some other way? I would estimate that on average teenagers think something negative about themselves every day. For some, this thinking could be constant.

Middle school and high school are times of transition. You're not in elementary school anymore, with parents watching over your shoulder every single minute, but you're not in college yet, living on your own.

You can make more decisions for yourself, but not all. You may get dropped off at the mall to hang out with your friends. You may date. You start to figure out who you are apart from your family.

Sometimes you might not like that someone very much. I was a shy kid. At least, I always thought of myself as shy. I was okay answering questions in class. I was able to talk to strangers and even gave speeches in front of crowds at youth group gatherings. My heart pounded beforehand and my underarms always sweat while I did it (which was way more embarrassing than the speeches themselves), but I could speak in front of crowds and talk to strangers. It wasn't impossible.

So why did I consider myself shy? I had friends. I didn't hide away in my room all the time. I didn't *feel* confident, though. I was the type of kid who always thought people were judging me. When I walked into a room, I assumed everyone was analyzing my clothing choices, my hair, my body, and how ridiculous it was that my voice trembled when I asked a question.

At the time, I told myself that people didn't like me. I knew it. My mind thought of every possible insult that my peers could possibly throw, and some that no one but me would ever dream up. That's why I acted shy—not because I was scared of what *was happening*, but because I was afraid of what *could happen*. I knew that hurt could come at any second, and I was ready to protect myself.

I slouched and blushed because I wanted to disappear. I believed that if I disappeared, nobody could recognize my faults.

I didn't take risks or ask what I considered "silly questions" because people might laugh at me. Call me names. Proclaim me a failure.

I thought I knew what everyone was going to say. And even when they didn't say it, I still heard those names in my head. I heard them loudly, even though *I* was the one insulting myself. *I* was the one causing myself all this misery and making myself pull away from the world.

Along with distress tolerance, another key skill I learned in treatment was cognitive reframing, a tool used in cognitive behavioral therapy. At its core, cognitive behavioral therapy is a treatment method that aims to lower your anxiety by changing your thoughts.

Cognitive reframing

Say you have a painting you think is ugly. Maybe it has lots of colors you don't like, all swirled together. It might be in an ugly frame, one that makes it look even more depressing. You might stick this picture in the corner of a room because it makes you sad to look at it. The picture might make the whole room, even the whole house, look worse.

But what happens when you switch the frame to one that makes the colors look better and balances out the scene? The picture still might not be your favorite thing to look at, but at least you won't cringe. At least it won't ruin your day or your house.

This is what cognitive reframing is: taking a thought that makes you feel awful about yourself and changing or rewording that thought to make it neutral, or even positive. To make the ugly picture—and your worldview—a little less awful.

Entire courses are dedicated to cognitive behavioral therapy, so you're obviously not going to become an expert through this chapter. Mastering cognitive reframing takes practice and time because it can be hard to realize that some of the messages you've been sending to yourself for your whole life are, in fact, a lie. They make so much sense in your head, after all!

How thoughts, feelings, and emotions are connected

Deep down, a part of your brain knows that the bad things you think about your weight and yourself may not be true. It's the same part that led you to pick up this book. It's the same part that believes in a life without disordered eating.

Your thoughts *are* important. But they are not always correct, such as when you think bad things about yourself. Somewhere inside of you, you know this. You know you are worthy. You know you are enough.

Cognitive behavioral therapy is based upon the idea that your thoughts, your feelings, and your actions are all inter-related. When you have a thought, a specific feeling is naturally going to follow. If you think something bad about yourself, you will probably feel bad. You may sink into a bad mood. You may isolate yourself from others. If you have a positive thought, however, you'll probably feel good. You may smile. Maybe you'll do a good deed. You may take a risk that pays off.

Cognitive behavioral therapy is about changing all three of these things: your thoughts, your feelings, and your behavior. If you change your thinking so that you feel good, you're more likely to do something that's good for you.

That's the positive side of the cycle. But what happens when your negative thought leads to a negative feeling? You might think something bad, feel bad, and then do something that hurts yourself, like engaging in disordered eating, purging, or too much exercise. You might think, *Why not? Everyone hates me already.*

That's the negative side of the cycle, which keeps repeating itself over and over again. As you engage in disordered eating and other harmful coping mechanisms, you'll start to feel bad. And so it goes, again and again, until recovery seems further and further away.

The cycle always completes itself. Thoughts lead to feelings, which lead to behaviors. Behaviors twist back around to more thoughts and feelings. If you don't take a step back and recognize how endless this cycle can be, you'll get stuck in it. You'll waste your entire life feeling not good enough or punishing yourself for something you didn't do wrong at all.

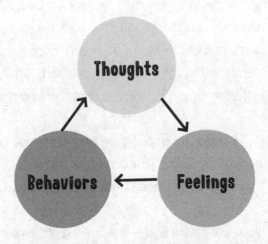

So how do you reframe your thoughts? And what if you don't believe yourself when you do it?

You might *not* believe yourself at first. That's the hard part. You may try to reframe a thought and *still* feel awful because you don't believe this reimagined truth in the slightest.

That doesn't mean that cognitive reframing will never work. You need practice and repetition to believe anything, especially statements that go against what you've seen as the truth for months or even years.

You can change your thoughts. You can change your behavior. Just take it one situation at a time.

For example, you might think, *I don't like what my body looks like. That means I'm a failure.*

At first, you might not realize there's anything to reframe here. If you think this, you may believe it's true. After all, why would your head lie to you? You may tell yourself that of course you're a failure if your body isn't "acceptable." You may accept the thought instantly. You may let it affect the rest of your day. You may engage in a destructive behavior.

But if you know about cognitive reframing, you can use these new skills instead; you can work on reframing that harmful thought so it doesn't affect your mood or your actions.

For you, your *reaction*—the feeling that you are a failure—is a distortion. It is based on the skewed logic of your eating disorder rather than the truth. When you have an eating disorder, many of your *feelings*, especially the anxious ones, are distorted and twisted by other people's comments, by your own feelings about your body, or by the messages we get from the media and society that however you look is "unacceptable."

Learning to accept others' opinions— even when they're negative

What would you think if your frenemy walked up to you and said, "Nice outfit"? Would you believe them? Or would your mind automatically jump to the conclusion that they're being sarcastic, that your outfit is hideous and that no one will ever like you?

I jumped to conclusions like that a lot. (And then I felt bad about myself all day, skipped dinner, and ran to punish myself.)

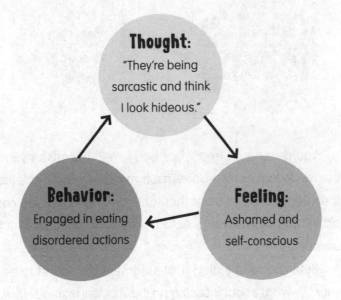

Thought:
"They're being sarcastic and think I look hideous."

Feeling:
Ashamed and self-conscious

Behavior:
Engaged in eating disordered actions

But what would happen if you chose to believe that person instead? If you said, "Thanks, I like this outfit, too." You'd probably feel happy. You might go on with your day that much more confident. You'd probably feel great and would treat your body well.

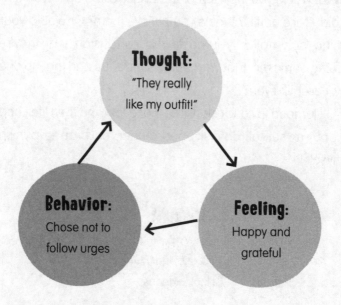

You deserve to treat your body well. Because even if some random person does insult you some day, that's just their opinion. Here is another tactic you can take: You can accept that someone *is* actually insulting or making fun of you.

But instead of letting that judgment run—and ruin—your life, what about focusing on this thought instead: *That's just their opinion.*

Those are four powerful words:

That's just their opinion.

Realizing the truth and meaning behind this sentence changed my life:

I don't have to care about what other people think.

Repeat it after me. (Or if it would be way too embarrassing to speak out loud right now, think it. You can say it later. You can say it all you want, for the rest of your life.)

I don't have to care about what other people think. I can't make everyone happy. This is just their opinion, and it's no better than mine.

Imagine how your life would change if you believed this. If you lived this.

You wouldn't have to buy certain brands of clothes because they're in fashion even though they're super uncomfortable.

You could act silly in the lunchroom without worrying what "people" will think about you.

You wouldn't have to join clubs or do sports you dislike simply to gain your peers' or your parents' approval.

You could have crushes on the people you like.

You could stop manipulating your body and let it be what it is meant to be.

You are your own person. Let other people judge themselves. *You* can judge you.

Or not.

Because that's what we're all learning here. What I'm still learning. I don't *have* to judge myself. It's not a requirement for being human.

When I start thinking that I'm a failure, when I look in the mirror and don't like how I look, I don't *have* to feel awful about it. I don't have to do anything to fix myself.

I am not my thoughts. No one is forcing me to obey them. I can stop, examine my thoughts, and make a decision on my own, based on what I want my future to look like. I may have to reframe my thoughts, but I never have to reframe myself.

I am enough. So are you.

EXERCISE: WATCHING YOUR THOUGHT CYCLE

Make a list of all the negative thoughts and judgments you may have in a half hour. See if you can trace these thoughts through the thought-feeling-behavior cycle. Try to think of a different thought you can substitute next time.

For example, if you look in the mirror and see a pimple on your nose, you might automatically think that you look ugly. But what if you substituted this thought instead: *Most people have to deal with pimples, so I'm not alone and this isn't a big deal.*

Instead of feeling bad about yourself and hiding from the world, you might realize that what you're going through is totally normal. You'll interact with people and smile. You'll have a good day instead of one shadowed by pimply clouds.

Maybe a classmate makes fun of you when you drop your tray in the cafeteria, which makes you automatically think that you're a loser and will never fit in.

But what if you instead told yourself that everyone makes mistakes? What if you laughed at yourself and maybe even took a bow? Instead of punishing yourself because one person might dislike you, you can tell yourself that everyone doesn't *have* to approve of what you do. And that anyone who dislikes you because you dropped a tray (or for any other reason!) isn't worth your time anyway.

What kind of examples can you think of in your life?

EXERCISE: CHANGING NEGATIVE THOUGHTS

If you can, try to change a negative thought the moment it occurs. What happens? Is it hard? After you changed the thought, did you end up doing something different from what you usually do after a negative thought?

CHAPTER 10
Why Relaxation Is Important

Relaxation can be hard

CLOSE YOUR EYES and take a deep breath. In and out. Now count to ten, slowly, and try not to let your mind wander. One, two, three . . .

Did you find that difficult? If so, you're not alone. Even though I know how important relaxation is, I'm awful at it. Forced relaxation, that is. I've tried meditation. I've tried yoga. I've tried the whole mindfulness thing where you stare at a raisin for a full minute to examine how it looks, then put it in your mouth to really experience the taste. At the time, this exercise felt extremely odd to me. It's a raisin. Can I just pop it in my mouth and get on with eating the next raisin?

As you can see, I have always struggled to relax. I still do today, but have found some techniques that work for me.

How I struggled with relaxation

When I was in treatment for my eating disorder, I did not know how to sit still. Part of this was because of my intense desire to burn off the calories I was ingesting, but most of this antsiness came from my anxiety. My treatment team (the set of doctors, nutritionists, and counselors at my treatment center) kept telling me to trust them—that everything would be okay when I followed the course of treatment—but I couldn't let myself believe them quite yet.

I didn't understand this new world I had stepped into, a world where what I thought was true was all wrong. Where I had to trust other people and my own body above all else.

I was afraid. I was scared. I wanted to run. At the very least, I wanted to bounce my leg up and down all day long. How was I supposed to do a silly relaxation exercise before a meal if my heart was pounding out of my chest? How would stretching and yoga make me feel better when I was used to running?

How? How? How?

Here's what I should have been saying: Yes. Yes. Yes.

Because my treatment team was right. (They usually were. I hated how that always happened. It's like how I got older and realized that my parents actually know what they're talking about.) I needed to relax and let go. Trust that someone would catch me when I fell. Trust that my *body* would catch me when I fell.

Relaxation is important for recovery

You know those free-fall trust exercises? The ones where you cross your arms over your chest, then fall backward without buckling or trying to save yourself? Where someone else has to catch you, someone you might not know very well, someone you might not even like very much?

That's what recovery is like. Standing tall and trusting. Leaning and not resisting. Trusting what you think shouldn't be trusted at all.

Relaxing into yourself and welcoming who you are with open arms. And if not with open arms, then at least by not pushing yourself and your feelings away.

Relaxing into yourself also means actually *relaxing*: doing something without distracting yourself with obsessions or the constant need to do more, move more, or achieve more.

Learning to be still

Relaxation is still hard for me. Even now, when I *don't* hate my body, when I *don't* think about weight loss every hour of every day, I still like to *do*. I like to get things done. I like to read as much as I can and work on my next book idea. I like to scroll through the latest news and see what my friends are talking about online. I like to be connected.

I'm still learning that it's okay to be disconnected. That simply being with myself is okay. That I don't have to multitask while I'm watching TV. (This is still a constant source of discussion between me and my husband, who gets irritated when I miss out on a piece of dialogue because I'm looking at my phone.) I don't have to scroll through social media or do a crossword puzzle at the same time as I watch a movie. There's no one keeping a scorecard of how much I get done in a certain day.

What are some ways you can relax?

You may be someone who always focuses on goals or achievement, but for me, doing something that makes me happy or relaxed is an achievement by itself.

People need relaxation. And relaxation can help you deal with your disordered eating. Here are a few ways to try to relax.

Yoga

Yoga forces you to slow down and be aware, to notice how the different parts of your body interact with each other and to see how, no matter what your size, you can move and flow and be strong. Many studies have found that doing yoga helps individuals grow to accept, if not love, their bodies. A twelve-week study of adolescent girls with eating disorders in 2016 showed that doing yoga led to a decrease in depression, anxiety, and concerns about weight and shape.[40]

Any size body can do yoga, too. In fact, a growing segment of the yoga community embraces and celebrates larger sizes. Many disabled people can do yoga; yoga positions can be modified according to a person's ability. If you're taking a yoga class, yoga teachers can help you come up with poses that are comfortable for you—they're trained in this.

Sleep

Sleep is pretty great, too. This may sound silly and oh so obvious, but every body needs sleep. Regular sleep keeps your brain working, heals your body and your heart, and helps with decision-making and regulating emotions. But many kids don't get the sleep they need. The National Sleep Foundation states that only 15 percent of teens reported sleeping for eight and a half hours on school nights. But teens need eight to ten hours of sleep per night to function at peak effectiveness and alertness.[41]

And, honestly, why wouldn't you want to be at peak alertness? Peak alertness is when you can experience life the most. When you're able to concentrate in school the best, remember what you studied for tests, and play hard during sports practice. Sleep is good. I like sleep.

Sleep is just as important as food and water. Sleep allows your muscles to heal from the activities of the day. It lets your brain consolidate memories and lets your body recharge.

The National Sleep Foundation states that when people drive while sleep-deprived, it's just as dangerous as driving drunk. The human body is *that* incapacitated by being overtired.[42]

Sleep is also an important part of recovery.

In her recovery, biology student Michelle has made self-care a priority despite her busy schedule. "I know that anxiety about food is heightened when I'm running on little sleep; I recognize that I tend toward restrictive behaviors during these periods," she said. "Recovery is maintaining a firm commitment to a stable sleep schedule, even when it's difficult because of social obligations or classes."[43]

Imagine what exhaustion does to your decision-making skills. You *need* to be alert when you're navigating a world that's trying to convince you that you're not enough the way you are.

Listening to your body applies to rest just as much as food. You are allowed to take a time-out from the world. Rest and relax so you can wake up as fully able to be kind to yourself as possible.

Mindfulness exercises

When you are aware of something, you are mindful of it.[44] You are present in the moment, feeling your feelings and accepting what is going on. Specific exercises can help you develop this quality of "mindfulness," which is often way harder than it sounds.

In theory, it should be easy to focus on one thing. But our minds wander a lot! We hear a noise and wonder what it is. We feel an itch on our elbow. Then we think about that thing our friend told us at lunch. We wonder what's for dinner. We wonder if we should eat something else for dinner instead.

Then, without even realizing it, we're not in the moment at all!

This does not mean that you've failed at mindfulness, though. Minds wander. Minds think. It is what they do. Mindfulness training teaches you to accept that your mind *will* wander and how to gently bring it back to what you are trying to focus on.

The raisin exercise I mentioned earlier is commonly used to help people think of food beyond its connection to weight and body. Food has a smell, taste, and texture. It can bring joy.

Deep breathing is another mindfulness exercise to help people center themselves. When your thoughts are spinning and you can't stop obsessing, trying to focus on one thing—your breathing—can help push those worries aside.

Being mindful can help with body acceptance because being mindful *is* being accepting: One can't exist without the other. Here's an exercise that will help you understand:

EXERCISE: CONNECT WITH YOUR BODY

Lie with your eyes closed and breathe in deeply. Listen to the noises around you. Feel your arms wherever they're resting. How do they feel? Feel your heels against the floor and your hair against your face. Which parts of your body feel tense? If your mind wanders, bring it back to the present moment, to your body.

During mindfulness exercises, you are not trying to determine the size or shape of your body or whether it's changed. Instead, these exercises are meant to help you notice your place in the world and to show you that you do not take up "too little" space or "too much" space. You are simply here, touching the earth and breathing in and out.

You are a person.

You are here.

You do not have to think about this morning or tomorrow.

You do not have to think about five minutes from now.

You are only in this single moment.

You don't have to do anything or achieve anything.

You are here and you are present.

There is no competition and no pressure.

There is just you.

Mindfulness can sound like a bunch of airy-fairy non-sense to some people. It sounded like that to me at first. But now I realize that it really *can* be helpful to take a break, to give myself permission—or have someone *else* give me permission—to step back and breathe.

Just breathe.

NOTE: If you cannot find or afford a meditation, mindfulness, or yoga class near you (or if you don't yet feel comfortable relaxing in front of a group), there are many apps that your parents can help you download for free or a low cost. YouTube has a number of meditation and relaxation videos you can follow along with. Many community centers often offer yoga and meditation classes at reduced rates, as do public libraries, which usually go one step further and offer classes for free!

EXERCISE: A PEACEFUL MINUTE

Stay still and quiet for a minute. You can sit, stand, or lie down for this, but you do have to be still. Breathing is all you have to do. Set a timer, then breathe in and out. Try to inhale for five seconds, then exhale for five seconds. Breathe in through your nose and out through your mouth, only focusing on those breaths. But breathe deeply. Let the air fill your whole lungs. This will mean that your stomach needs to expand out, but that's okay. Every time you think about something that's not your breathing, bring your mind back to those ins and outs.

How many times did your mind wander? Did this exercise make you uncomfortable or anxious? Why?

EXERCISE: OBJECT STUDY

Pick an object near you. The object doesn't have to be a raisin, but it should be something non-human. Focus on that object and describe it to yourself. What does it look like? Is it curved? Sharp? Smooth? What color is it? What shade? What purpose does it have? How does it look in comparison with other objects around it? If you can touch it, how does it feel? Smell? Is it something you can hear or taste?

When you're done, think about this object and its place in the world. Do you have a place, too—you with all your unique characteristics?

CHAPTER 11

Who's This "Ed" Guy? (One Way to Think About Your Eating Disorder)

It helps some people to think of their eating disorder as a person

FOR MANY PEOPLE dealing with eating disorders, "Ed" is the name they give their disease. It's a way to separate themselves from the voice in their head telling them to engage in disordered eating or exercise.

Ed is the whisper in their ear telling them they're not good enough, the scream yelling at them to do more and *be* more.

Author and eating disorder recovery advocate Jenni Schaefer talked about this imaginary Ed in her 2003 book *Life Without Ed*, which she expanded upon in its sequel, *Goodbye Ed, Hello Me*.

When I say "imaginary," I don't mean that Ed isn't real. I don't mean that he *is* real, either. (Or she, or whatever gender your Ed is. I use *he/him* pronouns here because that's how Jenni Schaefer refers to Ed.)

Ed is both real *and* "all in your head." That's because he's the voice *in* your head telling you to do things that you know will hurt your body. He's part of you, but he isn't the "true" you at all.

It sounds weird, right? The whole Ed thing sounds like something you'd never want to admit to another person, lest they think you're imagining things. You don't want to admit that you hear voices in your head.

I did, though. I still do, sometimes. They're soft as a whisper now, but every so often, when I'm stressed or down on myself, I hear them:

You're not a good person.

You'll never get all your work done.

You'll feel better if you go for a run.

Before, when I was really sick with my eating disorder, Ed's voice was louder. The whispers were more like yells. They were booming and overwhelming, like the sound of fire engines' sirens at a Fourth of July parade. Even if I put my hands over my ears, they were still there. Their echoes lasted, too, swirling around in my head until I had no choice but to obey, by engaging in disordered eating and exercise.

I was flooded with negative thoughts about myself. All those messages came from Ed. Ed is mean. Ed didn't like me. Ed didn't want me to recover. He didn't want me to like myself because then he'd have nothing to do. He'd be out of a job. And that would make Ed sad.

That's good, though. In recovery, your *job* is to make Ed sad.

Schaefer likes to look at Ed as a separate person, one you need to fight back against. One you don't need to listen to. You can think of Ed as a mean significant other or partner. Or a "friend" who doesn't have your best interests at heart. Ed can be like a grandparent who always pinches your cheeks and criticizes every little thing you do because your behavior isn't "proper enough."

Whoever Ed is, he's someone you don't want in your life. He's someone who makes you feel bad about yourself and who doesn't care about you. Why would you want to listen to someone who constantly criticizes and emotionally abuses you? Would you stand that kind of behavior from a friend?

I definitely wouldn't. I'd talk to my friend about how much of a jerk she was being. Then if she didn't change, she wouldn't have a place in my life.

That's why it can be helpful to distinguish Ed from ourselves. When you separate out the messages an eating disorder sends you—the messages you hear so often that they start to seem like reality—it can become easier to fight back against them.

It can be easier to yell at Ed to shut up.

How to talk to Ed

You can speak to Ed out loud. If you're alone in your room and it's helpful to literally tell Ed that he is wrong, go for it. Don't be embarrassed. Yell! Anything that helps you take your power back and show your eating disorder that you are the one in charge of your life. Even if you're not alone, you can still talk out loud.

You can also argue with Ed in your head. If your eating disorder tells you that you shouldn't keep eating according to your meal plan, you can retort back that your body needs fuel to live your life.

If your eating disorder tells you that life is too overwhelming and disordered eating will make you feel better, you can say that you have other ways to calm your emotions now.

If your eating disorder tells you that you can't hang out with your friends because you need to exercise, you can tell him that making memories is more important than a workout.

You can tell Ed that you're in charge.

Then you can imagine Ed disappearing in a puff of smoke.

In reality, it's not that easy. You won't always have a response for everything Ed throws at you because that guy is tricky. He's sneaky. He's aware of every single one of your weaknesses. If you're a creaky old house, Ed is the gust of wind that knows every single crack it can sneak into to make your life colder and colder.

Finding your voice amid the clamor of Ed's

If you keep separating out Ed's voice from your own, you'll get to know what he sounds like and what his common tricks are.

And if you keep challenging that little voice inside your head, you'll start to realize that Ed's words aren't orders you have to follow. They're actually really mean commentaries on your life that *you can choose to ignore*. That's right! You can disobey Ed. And the more you do, the easier it becomes. You'll be able to predict the types of things Ed might say and identify how those messages make you feel.

You'll be able to talk back and do the opposite action.

Maybe at first you'll only be able to identify Ed's messages. That's okay. It's still a step in the right direction.

Maybe at first you'll be able to talk back to the voice, but you won't be able to disobey it. That's okay, too.

Maybe you'll start doing things that go against what Ed wants, but then you'll feel guilty. You'll feel like you did something wrong. You'll feel full or you'll binge or you'll compare yourself with someone else and despair. You'll slip and go back to behaviors that you know aren't the healthiest.

That's okay. You can slip. Just as you can always pick yourself up again.

Because here's the important part—once you realize that Ed's messages are completely separate and different from the healthy actions you know will lead you toward a happy life, you can unlearn Ed's beliefs and start to follow healthier ones. You'll hear that voice in your head and know that it's Ed. And your Ed doesn't have to be human, either: For you, Ed may be a seven-fingered, purple-nosed alien from the planet Norblak.

You can picture Ed however you want. You just need to push Ed out of your life.

However you picture Ed, he doesn't have to be with you forever. If you don't want a purple-nosed alien in your life, you don't have to have one. You'd break up with someone who always calls you names, so why don't you do the same thing with Ed?

Remember, Ed may appear anywhere at any time: when you're eating with friends, when a caregiver criticizes your food choices, when your friends are busy on a Friday night and you're alone in your room, when you step onto the scale and the number isn't what you expected, or wanted, to see.

When you don't feel "enough."

That's not *your* voice yelling in your head. That's your eating disorder's. That's Ed's.

Talk back to him.

Yell at him.

Tell him that you won't listen. Then *don't* listen.

Over time, the voice will get quieter and quieter.

It may disappear entirely. It may not. But even if it doesn't, now that you know how it sounds, you never have to listen to that whisper again.

What if the idea of Ed doesn't work for you?

Sometimes the idea of Ed worked for me. Sometimes it was helpful to separate myself from my eating disorder and the mean messages it was giving me. If Ed was a different person, I could ignore him. I could banish him. Then I'd be *me* again. And if I was just me, I could be healthy. I wouldn't be sick or anxious or have people worried about me anymore.

That never happened, though, even when I made a conscious effort to identify the eating disorder voice. When I made a list of things Ed said and combated those insults and orders with my healthy voice, the anxieties and fears were still there. When I did the direct opposite of what Ed wanted, I was still afraid.

I didn't know why. Was I doing things wrong? Was my Ed different from everyone else's? Was I never going to recover?

I thought I was broken.

I wasn't broken; I was recovering. One super annoying thing is that recovery doesn't happen instantaneously. Even once you make the decision that you want to get better, that life with an eating disorder is unbearable, and that you'd rather do something scary than live one more day hungry and weight-obsessed—even then, there are ups and downs and steps backward.

Recovery is a process. It can take months. It can take years. All in all, the "official" length of my eating disorder and recovery—from when I started to diet and worry about my weight to when I finally let go of the teeny-tiny "I don't really think this is a problem because people without eating disorders do stuff like this, too" behaviors that kept me stuck in "almost recovery"—was twelve years.

Twelve years! That's a long time. Of course, every second of those twelve years wasn't misery. My sickness during that time took various levels of intensity, from "in the hospital" sick to "a healthy weight but still not letting myself have exactly what I want to eat" sick to "still wanting to be perfect" sick.

Recovery *isn't* perfect. Recovery isn't a straight line. As I mentioned before, recovery is ups and downs and squiggles and U-turns and doubling back. It's making progress, then getting scared and retreating back to your shell of safety.

Your eating disorder feels safe to you. It may not be fun, and it may make you miserable and sad, but it still feels safe. You know what to expect when you're dieting and purging and planning what to do each day. You're good at being body-obsessed. Your body can be controlled.

Recovery can't be controlled. Yes, there are meal plans and appointments and schedules you have to follow. There's accountability. And for many of you, there's nagging. There are people watching you to make sure you do the right thing.

But you can't predict how you're going to feel every day in recovery. Some mornings you might wake up ready to take on the world and show your eating disorder who's boss. Some mornings you might wake up, look in the mirror, and immediately feel gross. You may immediately want to do "something" to fix yourself, even though there is probably nothing to fix at all.

So if Ed doesn't work for you, try not to feel bad about it. Ed is a helpful concept for a lot of people. But if you don't like to think of Ed as a separate entity outside of yourself, that's okay, too. This idea doesn't work for everyone. Some people like to think of this Ed voice as *part* of them, something that's linked to who they are and their unique personality.

EXERCISE: THE THINGS ED SAYS

Make a list of all the things Ed says to you in a day. If you feel able to, respond to them in a way that you consider healthy. Which of Ed's messages could you ignore in the future? What would be some kinder things to say to yourself instead?

CHAPTER 12
Admitting Struggles and Being Vulnerable

It's okay to realize that you need help

IT'S HARD TO admit that you're wrong.

It's hard to admit that you don't know what you're doing.

It's hard to admit that you're flawed and not "as good as" everyone else.

As humans, we try to avoid this state of "wrongness" from the time we're little kids. We draw on the wall with marker and emphatically declare that it wasn't us, even when ink is smudged all over our hands. We vehemently shake our heads after throwing a ball in the house and accidentally knocking over a parent's favorite vase. Of course we didn't do that; it was just the wind. Oh, the window wasn't open? Well, then it was a ghost. Totally a ghost.

We deny because we don't want to get in trouble, but we also deny because we don't want to disappoint people. We don't admit when we're having trouble. We don't admit when we need help.

My eating disorder happened gradually, and I didn't think I could ask for help

When I was first getting sick with an eating disorder, it didn't happen all at once. I didn't decide that I wanted to lose weight and then all of a sudden start starving myself. It was more gradual than that. I ate a little less and exercised a little more. I got positive feedback for these actions and realized that I felt more in control of my life.

So I kept going. Soon, though, I realized that the things I was doing *weren't* actually making me feel better. They weren't making my life better, but now they were compulsions—they had taken control of me.

After a while, after I became really sick, I *couldn't* make myself eat more. I *couldn't* make myself exercise less. Even when I realized how miserable I was and decided I wanted to get better—I couldn't stop myself. It was as if my brain and my heart lived in two different dimensions; they spoke two different languages and couldn't communicate, no matter how hard I tried to make myself act in a healthy way.

I don't want to be sick anymore, I told my body and my mind. *Stop!*

I couldn't stop. If I tried to eat more, I felt a tightening in my chest. My body seized up and panic overtook me. If I stopped just one minute short of my regular exercise session, my body expanded. I had gained one hundred pounds in that one minute, I was sure of it, even though that statement made no logical sense whatsoever.

I knew that I needed help to get better, but I couldn't bring myself to ask for that help. If I asked for help, it would mean that I wasn't the perfect student/perfect daughter/perfect girl I was supposed to be—the one everyone always thought I was. I'd destroy that illusion. And without that illusion, who would I be? I'd be the girl with a mental illness, the one who couldn't do something as simple as eat on her own.

I couldn't let anyone think that. I couldn't be "that girl."

So instead I was the *other* girl. The girl who struggled alone. The girl who canceled plans and lost her friends because she didn't want them around. If they were around, they would see that something was wrong. They'd ask questions.

I became the girl who suffered in silence and didn't let anyone inside. The one who missed out on parties and dates and late-night chats because she was afraid of being found out. I didn't let anyone in, so nobody came in. I was alone.

I eventually got found out, of course, when my dad

busted me on the exercise bike in the middle of a work day. Before that, my parents had probably picked up on some clues. They saw me eating smaller meals and losing weight. They questioned if I was *really* going to eat breakfast on the way to school or if I'd *really* gone out for dinner with friends. They had all the puzzle pieces, but they hadn't put them together. They didn't see the whole picture yet, but that day, my dad stumbled upon the last piece, and my parents saw what had been there all along: a very sick daughter.

That's when I went into treatment for the first time. That's when therapists and counselors and nutritionists encouraged me to tell them what was going on, to let them know what I was afraid of. They told me to journal about my fears and struggles and speak up in groups about how hard this whole "recovery thing" was.

I didn't do any of those things. Even though I had been pulled out of school, even though I was staying overnight in the hospital, even though I was obviously sick, I was still afraid of telling people that I was having trouble.

Of course I was having trouble. Duh! (Remember, even if you don't go into treatment, you can still be having trouble. There is no achievement you need to reach before you can ask for help.)

I didn't want to *say* I was sick, though. Saying the words and admitting that I had a problem would make it real. And I didn't want to make it real, even as I was discharged from the hospital and then almost immediately sent back again because I had relapsed.

I didn't have a problem. (So I ate my new meal plan and smiled the whole time.)

I didn't have a problem. (So I told people how easy things were and how much better I was getting.)

I didn't have a problem. (So I kept relapsing.)

In my mind, I wasn't smiling. Eating food and stopping all exercise wasn't easy. It hurt my body, and it made my mind anxious. I didn't want to do it in treatment, and I didn't want to do it when I left.

I didn't tell anyone this, though. I didn't want them to know that I wasn't the perfect girl or the perfect patient. And because I didn't tell anyone, no one could help me.

That's why I relapsed. Not because recovery is hard. (It *is* hard, yes, but it's *impossible* without being open about things.) I relapsed because I wasn't honest. I wasn't vulnerable. The only way to make recovery easier—to make recovery possible—is to talk about it, to discuss the hard parts and to get help wading through them.

I was in and out of treatment a lot before I was honest with myself. It took even longer before I was honest with my doctors and my nutritionist. I was ashamed to be sick. Ashamed to be broken. Afraid to be vulnerable. So I kept all my struggles inside. And they grew and grew and grew.

I hid things like this a lot. I still hide my true feelings

sometimes, in areas that don't have anything to do with food. It's hard to admit that I'm not keeping up with everything. That some days I get randomly sad. That every single laundry basket in the house is overflowing. That I canceled dinner with my friend last week because I was so stressed out about other things.

I do get sad, though. I do make mistakes.

I'm human.

You might feel scared and alone, but it's okay to reach out

It might be the same for you.

If you've recently changed schools, is it hard to admit that the new building is way too big and kind of scary?

If you can't understand something that's going on in class but every single other person seems to know instinctively what's going on, do you hesitate before raising your hand and asking for an explanation? Do you ask for an explanation at all?

If you didn't make the softball team and your parents were expecting you to, are you afraid to tell them?

If you get dumped, is it hard to tell your friends?

If you get teased every day at school, do you tell a parent? Or do you let your family keep thinking that you're the most popular kid in school?

Why?

Why is it so hard to admit that we have problems? Why is it so hard to admit that we struggle and fall and fail and hurt?

Everyone hurts. Everyone falls. It might not seem that way, but I promise that every single kid in your grade has some sort of problem. Their problems might not be as bad as yours, and they might not be having them right now, but every person still has problems. No one's life is perfect.

Let me repeat that: No one's life is perfect.

You aren't expected to be perfect, either. In fact, when you pretend to be perfect, as I did, when I wouldn't tell anyone that I was sick or when I told everyone that recovery was all sparkles and unicorns—well, then you just end up hurting even worse.

I often wonder what would have happened if I had told people that I was struggling with food and recovery. That I was worried about my body and couldn't make myself eat more, even though my stomach was angrily demanding to be fed. Maybe I wouldn't have been sick for as long as I was.

Maybe. Maybe not.

I don't know. What I do know is that in my life now I try my best to be honest. I don't always succeed. I might have a bad day and tell my mother that things are fine when she asks because I really don't want to get into the details. I might tell my husband that I'm okay, even though I woke up feeling anxious for some reason.

These are little things, though, and I do them so that my loved ones won't worry. But if these little things ever become *big* things, I know it's time for me to open my mouth and tell the truth.

I am vulnerable. I hurt. I make mistakes, lots of them.

I am still worthy, though. Even when I was sick, I was worthy. People didn't think less of me because I asked them for help. They thought more of me, actually. They respected me for speaking up. They *wanted* to help.

What if you don't know where to turn for help?

If you don't think that you have anyone in your life right now who can help you, please keep looking. So many communities are out there waiting with open arms to let you in. There are support groups for queer kids and teens. There are groups specifically for boys with eating disorders and groups for specific ages. There are teachers and adults and peers who are willing to listen and help if your home life feels unstable.

You can and will find people who can help, whether it's helping you recover and get your disordered eating under control or simply listening to you cry about losing a relationship or failing a test. If they matter—if they're worth it—people will listen.

They will help.

EXERCISE: THE THINGS YOU'RE AFRAID TO SAY

What are some things you're afraid to tell people about yourself? If it's hard to write these things down, list them in your head. For each item, write what you think would happen if you told people about it. What would they say? Do? How would you feel? How would telling someone help?

If you can, choose one thing you're struggling with and choose someone to confide in. Plan out what you're going to say. You can even preface the talk with how you're nervous. What happens?

PART THREE

Society, Role Models,
Family, and Media

CHAPTER 13

BMI and Why It's Nonsense

Why BMI exists

ONE FLAWED MEASUREMENT that doctors—and society—obsess over is BMI.

Body mass index is a calculation that a lot of people think is important, but that doesn't actually show much about a person's overall health. It's just a number determined by your weight and height. The theory is that by looking at this ratio, doctors will be able to screen more easily for people at risk for potential health problems.

So depending on this number, people are sorted into categories: "underweight," "normal weight," "overweight," or "obese." If someone is "obese" or "overweight," that person may be perceived as being less healthy than someone who's a "normal" weight. If people are a "normal" weight, they may be seen as being more healthy.

But the truth is that BMI is arbitrary. The classifications are arbitrary. So arbitrary, in fact, that in 1998 the BMI scale was changed, lowering the cutoffs for each category and instantly reclassifying millions of once "normal weight" people as "overweight" or "obese."[45]

"Obese" is a made-up label

How would our world and the way we feel about ourselves change if we didn't have to lose weight? If "obese" people weren't *expected* to lose weight?

People who are considered "obese" can be healthy. They can have normal blood pressure and a healthy heart. People who are considered "obese" can also be ill.

Thin people can get sick, too, just as thin people can be healthy.

This is why it's important for medical professionals to focus on the individual. What is that *one* specific patient experiencing? What are the individual's symptoms, regardless of body size? How can those symptoms be treated?

Our society needs to stop demonizing certain body types. Healthy or not, in shape or not, everyone deserves care and respect.

In this book I only use "obese" (in quotation marks) as an official medical term. Many activists prefer *fat* as the descriptive word, so I choose to use it instead. "Fat" is not a description of anything bad, just as body size is not a determinant of self-worth.

When someone uses the BMI scale to define someone as "obese," though, they reduce people to a single number that doesn't necessarily mean anything about their health or the medical care that they need. Many people use medical terms to have an excuse to discriminate against a certain group, claiming that fatness leads to unhealthiness—even though the science doesn't necessarily support that.

A doctor may say that someone is "obese" or "overweight." "Obese" and "overweight" are not character flaws. Writing these words down on a medical chart doesn't make that particular patient unable to live their lives. BMI is one metric that health professionals use and, when taken in conjunction with other factors, doesn't mean much at all.

In her book *Body of Truth*, professor and author Harriet Brown explains that BMI as a concept has been around for a long time; it was invented by a mathematician in the 1830s for analyzing large groups of people, not individuals. The mathematician was curious about what the "average man" looked like. He wanted to describe and compare different groups, not judge and demonize certain people. To him, the number was a description, not a way to measure morality.[46]

That all started to change in the 1970s, when researchers started using BMI to compare people's sizes in the name of health. But the most serious shift came in 1998, when the weight categories were changed altogether, immediately redefining many more people as "overweight" or "obese." That's when the hysteria began—when we started to hear reports about an "obesity crisis."

A 2016 study published in the *International Journal of Obesity* concluded that after reviewing more than forty thousand people's health data, 47 percent of people classified as "overweight" were healthy based on all other measures, as were 30 percent of people classified as "obese" and 16 percent of people classified as "extremely obese."[47] Seventy percent of people classified as "normal" weight were healthy based on other measures. That's a lot of healthy people across all categories.

Some problems with BMI

BMI has a ton of limiting factors. For one thing, it only considers weight in relation to height. It doesn't measure the composition of that weight, whether it's dense, compact muscle or fluffier fat, nor does the calculation take into account the size of a person's frame.

This means that athletic people could be classified "overweight," and seen as less healthy, simply because they have more muscle. In fact, the BMI scale classifies many high-level athletes, who are in better shape than basically everyone else in the world, as "overweight"—or even "obese."

An NPR article from 2016 noted that "based on players' height and weight on the NFL website, there is no Denver Broncos player with a normal BMI."[48] Should these athletes be demonized because of their weight? Of course not. Should we be worried about their weight? No.

But you don't need to flash a Super Bowl ring to "excuse" your BMI. Most of us will never be sports superstars. But we shouldn't be discriminated against, either. We shouldn't have to analyze our frame to defend our BMI.

We need to take any consideration of BMI out of the equation altogether.

Blogger and singer-songwriter Katie Zeitz talked to me about how her eating disorder wasn't noticed for a long time because her weight was "normal," according to the BMI chart. "I'm naturally quite curvy, though," she said, so even though the *numbers* told everyone she was fine, she was still engaging in disordered behaviors to get there. She was still suppressing her body's intended weight and frame.[49]

EXERCISE: BEYOND BMI

Do you obsess over your weight, clothing size, or BMI? Try to stop thinking about those numbers, and instead, think about things that make you happy. Try making a list as you think about other aspects of you: What do you like about yourself? What do you enjoy doing? What makes you feel good?

CHAPTER 14

Why You Should Ignore the Media's "War on Obesity"

How is "obesity" used to scare us?

WHEN YOU WATCH the news, they're always there—insulting and dehumanizing pictures of "overweight" people. Stories about restaurants listing calorie counts so they can save citizens from themselves. The jokes about fat people. Stories about the mistreatment of fat people. The supposedly well-meaning suggestions or comments about how "if they only ate less and exercised more . . ."

All of these messages are so easy to absorb.

Jes Baker, body positive activist and blogger at *The Militant Baker*, said in her 2014 TEDx Talk that young girls are more afraid of getting fat than they are afraid of cancer, war, or losing their parents.[50]

Let that sink in. Many people are more afraid of *fat* than of disease and death. But what are they so scared of?

Alexis Johnson, an undergraduate student who was diagnosed at the age of twenty with Other Specified Feeding and Eating Disorder (OSFED), recalls seeing food documentaries like *Super Size Me* and *Food Inc.* during her adolescence. She said that these movies and other media "drove a lot of fear-based dialog around health, wellness, and food consumption," and she started to internalize these messages.[51]

"I think society has heavily influenced the fear I experience in relation to food, eating, and my body . . . I was so scared of becoming obese," she said, "or getting diabetes, or becoming some other health statistic."

Because of society's fixation on "clean eating," it can be difficult to let go of misconceptions about food and eating that might contribute to orthorexic behaviors. "Even now," said biology student Michelle, "although I think I'm in a healthy place, I have to consciously stop myself from feeling like I need to scold or reward myself based on what food I'm eating."[52]

It might seem ironic that health concerns would lead to unhealthy and disordered behavior, but for Johnson, Michelle, and many others, the media's hyper-focus on "obesity" does just that.

Misinformation about weight leads to underdiagnosis

Society shames people for their weight—particularly fat people and anyone in the "overweight" or "obese" category of the body mass index. (See more on how BMI is a flawed measurement in Chapter Thirteen.) People are told that they can't possibly have an eating disorder if they are "overweight." To make matters worse, sometimes insurance companies won't cover treatment if a person is at or above what they consider "ideal body weight."

Doctors at the Mayo Clinic in Rochester, Minnesota, have noted that a significant number of adolescents considered "overweight" and "obese" seek treatment for eating disorders but that their symptoms were underdiagnosed and their weight loss behaviors were actually encouraged.[53]

A 2016 study looking at 9,713 college students found that "overweight" or "obese" students were at the highest risk for eating disorders.[54]

But many people don't recognize eating disorders in people who aren't underweight.

When graduate student and mental health advocate Melissa Martini got sick, both a family member and her therapist refused to accept that she had an eating disorder, because she was underweight, but not "dangerously" underweight.[55]

"I tried to tell a close family member that I was sick, but he only told me that my obsession with losing weight was a good thing because I'd always look good and be skinny. It made me feel as though he'd rather me look good than be alive.

"I was left feeling like I wasn't good enough at being sick, so what was the point of trying to recover?" Martini said. When Martini wasn't taken seriously by her therapist, either, she started thinking that she needed to get even worse before she could possibly get better: "If I get sick enough, maybe someone will finally notice and help me."

Many people physically *can't* get "skinny enough" for their eating disorders to be noticed. People are genetically programmed to be within a certain weight range.[56] This doesn't change, no matter how hard you work.

If you don't fit the "eating disorders stereotype" and you overexercise or engage in other harmful behaviors, your actions may be ignored or even encouraged because society doesn't *expect* to find eating disorders in people who are fat.

Society *expects* people to be dieting.

However, harmful behaviors are harmful to *any* type of body. Suppressing a body's true weight isn't healthy for *anyone*. And when an experience isn't recognized, accepted, or validated, the sad result is that certain groups of people don't get treatment.

In the end, society deems the idea of weight loss more important than the suffering of actual human beings.

It doesn't help that making people feel bad about being fat is a big business: In 2016, the weight loss industry was worth $66.3 billon.[57] That's a huge amount of money: It's almost six times more money than the film industry's box office revenue in the United States and Canada that same year.[58] Companies have a lot to gain by telling people that they should lose weight.

The fat acceptance movement started in the 1960s to fight discrimination against fat people.[59] Though many fat activists still advocate for its original values (protecting the rights of people with fat bodies and stopping bias), a lot of the online conversation about bodies is now centered around the body positive movement, which claims that every body is beautiful but often still advocates for dieting and other unhealthy behaviors.

"Obviously, all bodies are good bodies!" Marie Southard Ospina told Revelist in "Fat Acceptance Activists Explain Why Body Positivity Is Becoming Meaningless." "But the focus is no longer on the people who need it most: On the ones that society, by and large, does not treat as good."[60]

In the same article, fat acceptance writer Your Fat Friend noted: "As body positivity has become more mainstream, so has the concept of fat shaming. Unfortunately, the majority of media attention on fat shaming has focused on thin women inaccurately being called fat. Being called fat can cause real emotional pain for some, and many experience it as bullying. But when you *are* fat, that bullying is institutionalized, cemented in policies, and often publicly condoned."

Any teasing or harassment because of your body size is hard to endure. But for people who are fat, that bullying can prevent people from getting treatment.

Author, lecturer, and fat activist Virgie Tovar started her first diet when she was about eight, and began starving herself when she was eleven. But since she was bigger than the other kids, no one realized she was hurting her body.[61]

"As I was starving myself and working out obsessively, no one asked what I was doing," Tovar said. "My doctor didn't care that I was doing unhealthy things. His bias led him to congratulate me instead. And doctors can't help their patients if they have internalized fat phobia." If society automatically thinks that "fat equals bad," dangerous weight loss behaviors will be ignored or overlooked.

Constant dieting can be seen as a manageable way for fat people to lose weight and is often encouraged. Yet it's still within the spectrum of disordered eating, Tovar stressed.

"It's all about the mindset, about believing that you're 'bad' and taking it out on your body."

Tovar is still fat. She is proud of herself and her body. She credits this to a supportive community of feminists (remember, feminists can be any gender!) who taught her that anyone can be beautiful, who propped her up and complimented her when she was feeling down, and who taught her to stand up to society's messages.

Being underweight is dangerous, and having an eating disorder can be deadly

It is true that "obesity," as defined by the medical profession, can come with its dangers. Studies have said that it can raise the risk of heart disease, stroke, and diabetes. It can impair daily functioning, particularly because a lot of the world (airline seats and many desks, for example) is set up in a way that excludes fat people.

However, "overweight" individuals can be just as healthy as individuals of "normal weight" and are often even *healthier* than those who are "underweight."[62]

Being underweight can be very dangerous—even deadly.

In fact, studies show that the eating disorder anorexia nervosa, which causes many people to be malnourished, increases the risk of death by nearly six times, the highest mortality risk of any mental illness. This means that a person with anorexia is six times more likely to die than someone of the same age in the general population. And for those first diagnosed in their twenties, the risk is *eighteen* times greater.[63] (This is another argument for getting help sooner rather than later.)

Two common eating disorders, anorexia and bulimia, have significant dangers.

Here are some of their complications:[64]

- Heart problems, including reduction in its size, slow or irregular heart rhythm, and heart failure
- Low blood sugar, leading to fainting spells
- Loss of menstruation or irregular periods, leading to fertility problems
- Low testosterone in males
- Loss of bone density, increasing risk of bone breaks
- Organ failure
- Seizures
- Blood disorders, including anemia and severely low levels of Vitamin B-12
- Reduction in the brain's gray matter, affecting muscle control, sensory perception, and memory
- Dry skin and hair
- Hair loss and downy hair growth elsewhere on body

- Severe dehydration, leading to life-threatening low potassium levels
- Upset stomach and other digestive problems
- Damaged tooth enamel
- Water retention or bloating
- Ruptured esophagus

With those risks in mind, it's shocking that so much time is spent talking about the dangers of "obesity," when being underweight or having an eating disorder can be so hazardous.

There's nothing wrong with being fat

As you embark upon your recovery journey, you may gain weight. You may have to buy an entirely new wardrobe. If you are underweight, you will need to gain fat on your body to become healthy—and you will be uncomfortable for a while before you learn to accept your new body. It's unsettling to let your body find its own weight, to not control something after gripping it tightly for so long. It's scary to let your body make the decision *for* you—no input from you required, no work on your part needed.

You may not be 100 percent satisfied with your "recovery weight." You may feel strange in your body at first.

Angie Manfredi, a youth services librarian who blogs at *Fat Girl, Reading*, identifies as fat. She is not ashamed of the term.

"No one, no one anywhere in the world, even identical twins, does anything the exact same way. Maybe I can't do the same things that other people can—but then maybe I can do things *they* can't. Maybe some of those things are because of my size, but so what? Your size, your weight—these are just two parts of *you*. Find out what you can do because you *love* it, because it *interests* you, because it seems *fun* and figure out how your weight and size can make it work."[65]

Ragen Chastain, a speaker, writer, and activist who blogs at *Dances with Fat*, said the same thing:

"I spent a lot of years making lists of things that I was going to do just as soon as I got thin. Then one day I got fed up with that (and realized, based on the research, that it was highly unlikely that I would ever be thin) and so I decided to take my fat body out for a spin. Some things I was good at, some I wasn't, and that's because all bodies have abilities and limitations and mine is no exception. I have about as much chance of manipulating my body size as I do manipulating my height, so just as I don't try to make myself taller so that I can reach the top shelf, I don't try to make myself smaller so that I can run faster. If I want to work on something physical, then I work on strength, stamina, flexibility and/or technique and let my body size settle where it will."[66]

As of 2018, Chastain holds a Guinness World Record as the heaviest person ever to complete a marathon.

To Chastain, "the idea that I should try to get thin to escape fat shaming is akin to suggesting that I should give the bullies my lunch money so they stop beating me up. Anyone who was bullied knows that doesn't work."

Don't blame your body. Blame the alarmist media stories instead.

Manfredi stressed how important fighting back against these messages was in her own journey: "When you get messages from *anyone* or *anywhere* that you're less of a person because of your weight or your body, you need to remember that these messages simply aren't true, they aren't the whole story of what makes you who you are. Treat yourself with the same kindness and love you give the people you care about, and remember that hurtful, damaging messages aren't the only voices that matter."[67]

Chastain emphasizes that "the ability to see beauty is a skill set—we are all beautiful, but some people haven't developed their skill set sufficiently to see it."[68] It takes time to realize that all bodies are beautiful and that health and body size are two separate things.

You can work to get to the point where you realize—where you truly believe—these things, too.

There are so many types of bodies, any of which has the ability to be healthy or unhealthy. And no matter whether you are fat or thin, healthy or unhealthy, you deserve to live without being judged by other people—or by yourself.

EXERCISE: WHAT WOULD YOU DO IF YOU COULD CHOOSE?

Write about what kinds of food you'd eat and what types of activities you'd do if you (not your guilt, not the media, not your parents, not your friends) could choose. What foods and activities would you avoid? If your disordered eating wasn't a factor, would you live your life like this all the time? How would that make you feel?

CHAPTER 15
Puberty and Body Diversity

What is puberty?

WHEN MOST PEOPLE reach a certain age (usually between the ages of eight and thirteen for girls and between nine and fifteen for boys), their bodies undergo puberty. It's important to note that not everyone experiences puberty at the same time. Additionally, some people may take puberty blockers for health reasons like gender dysphoria or precocious puberty. No matter when a person experiences it, puberty is the process a person's body undergoes as it matures and develops.

It may be natural, but it's still difficult

Puberty starts at different times for different people. It is not certain what exactly determines the start of puberty, but some factors are body weight, hormones, and genetics. If people in your family all tend to go through puberty at a certain age, it is more likely that you will follow that same pattern.

For those who start puberty earlier than others, these changes can exacerbate the already difficult parts of adolescence. If you go through puberty earlier than your classmates, you may feel self-conscious. If you go through puberty later, you may think that you're the only one who's still a little kid. If you're transgender, maybe you're taking puberty blockers and not experiencing puberty yet.

One thing to remember is that pretty much everyone goes through puberty at some point. Some undergo these changes earlier, and some go through them later. But everyone's body *will* develop, whether early or late or somewhere in the middle. Our bodies don't all follow the same schedule. Our bodies don't all end up looking the same.

Everyone is different. What *is* the same is that our bodies change, whether in puberty or for some other reason. We are not robots. We do not stay the same size and shape forever. We are meant to change and we are meant to grow.

When other people have feelings about your body

Undergraduate student Alexis Johnson, who is multiracial, describes how having a "different" body made her feel like she couldn't live up to the ideals of her community.[69]

"Coming from a mixed background, but living in a fairly homogenous area, I never looked like any of my friends/peers," she said. "Going through adolescence was a rough experience because even though everyone's bodies were changing, mine was always going to be more different."

Not looking like the popular girls in her class because of her racial background damaged her self-image.

She said that as her body changed, she had a hard time adjusting to the changes. "I was desperate to cover up and hide myself," she recalled.

And to make matters worse, Johnson doubted her own struggles because she didn't fit the stereotypical image of a girl with an eating disorder.

"I was in denial for many years about having an eating disorder," she said, "because a couple of my classmates had eating disorders and fit the stereotypical look of someone with an eating disorder."

Johnson's classmates were both white teenage girls who were underweight and had received treatment at a residential recovery program.

"Since my experience did not fit that," she said, "I thought that I was 'in the clear.'" In fact, because of her skewed image of what someone with an eating disorder looked like, she didn't realize she had one until she learned about them in a college nutrition class.

For girls and many people assigned female at birth, part of puberty can be looking more "adult," which can be upsetting and can attract unwanted attention.

Shanetta McDonald, author of "How I Finally Admitted That My 'Quick Fix' Was an Eating Disorder," wrote that "eating disorders don't discriminate, and navigating the world as a bulimic African-American woman is tough. We're portrayed as strong women—women who believe Black is beautiful, and filled with pride of our ancestral curves. We're supposed to appear confident and have it pulled together. In my experience, this was true in every area of my life—except when it came to my body."[70]

She said that the people around her praised and accepted curves. But since she "didn't want to be seen" when she was younger, she tried to avoid this body type. "Having curves drew unwanted attention to me, both from my family and the outside world," McDonald said.[71] It was only by opening up about her behavior to a doctor and then a therapist that McDonald learned she didn't have to change her body.

"The hardest part was to love and accept my body, just as it is. I still struggle with this, but the negative thoughts and narrative that my disease tells me is much, much quieter. I had dieted and tried to change my body for most of my life, so of course it would take time for me to accept it! Today, I work on being gentle, kind, loving, and accepting of my body, no matter what."

Gender and puberty

There are lots of ideals out there for how people with binary genders should look, such as curves and breasts for women and muscles for men. Standards can extend beyond this focus on body shapes to what babies should wear and what activities children should participate in. For example, many people dress girls in pink and boys in blue, while giving girls dolls and boys trucks to play with. Society often has a specific idea of what our bodies and our interests should be.

But those standards do not apply to everyone, and may be particularly difficult or harmful to those who are genderqueer, nonbinary, or trans and are grappling with gender dysphoria. Your distress could be caused by your own body (if something about your body conflicts with your actual gender), often called physical dysphoria, or by society (such as a nonbinary person forced to use either a men's or women's restroom[72]), which is called social dysphoria.

Author Katherine Locke, whose pronouns are *they/them*, talked to me about how they grew up in a community where they didn't know any queer people. "No one talked about it, and it didn't seem to be an option. I think, in retrospect, that not understanding my feelings contributed to my eating disorder because it was a way to make my body and world understandable in a way. Additionally, I now identify as nonbinary or genderqueer, something I didn't even know was *possible* until late in college, or right out of college. I think that some of my eating disorder was an attempt to make my body match what I felt my gender was, without that language. The eating disorder *was* my language for that gender dysphoria for many years."[73]

For Locke, recovery came as they began to "accept that I had the right to exist and take up space as I was, even though I grew up in a world where queer bodies didn't exist or take up space."

Jamie Bushell, whose pronouns are *they/them*, expressed a similar viewpoint.[74] Bushell examines the queer perspective on eating disorder recovery as coauthor of the blog *ThirdwheelED*.

After treatment for an eating disorder in 2017, Bushell realized that they are nonbinary and that being queer made the blogger feel "like I wanted to hide and disappear and like my body wasn't worth being seen." Bushell's identity and body clashed so much that they didn't feel safe in either. "This struggle to express this part of me has kept me from being present in my life," they noted.

In a 2017 article for *HuffPost*, Bushell also stressed how hard it is for nonbinary or trans people to constantly hear the message that everyone needs to accept and love their bodies. "Body acceptance doesn't work with gender dysphoria," they wrote.[75]

Problems can also arise for trans people if they undergo hormone replacement therapy, which is sometimes called a "second puberty" and can intensify body awareness and anxiety.

"Growing up, I thought that if I could curb my appetite, I would also curb those feelings that I wasn't quite right, that something inside me didn't match my outside. I hoped that if there were less of me, there would be less of me that felt wrong," wrote children's librarian and author Kyle Lukoff (whose pronouns are *he/him*) in his essay for the anthology *Gender Outlaws: The Next Generation*.[76]

As Lukoff began to transition, he began to combat these feelings of wrongness even more: "It's not surprising that my eating disorder spiraled out of control when I began to transition physically. Trans folk are told we do not and should not exist, and when we do exist we must make every effort to assimilate."

Even when Lukoff was hospitalized, the people who were helping him were ignorant about how his trans history and gender identity could be related to eating disorders.

Luckily, many medical professionals are working to give

queer people the care they deserve. For example, in 2017, Walden Behavioral Care in Waltham, Massachusetts, launched a program that specifically treats LGBTQ people with eating disorders.

No matter what, it's important to remember that if you're dealing with gender dysphoria, you're not alone.

In my interview with Locke, they emphasized a message of love and welcome. "You are worthy of love," Locke said. "There's a queer community out here ready to embrace you, and a lot of us have been through the eating disorder ringer, too. We're here for you, any time you need us."[77]

CHAPTER 16

Who Are You Outside of Your Body?
Do You Think You Should Be
Like Everyone Else?

When the focus on appearance begins

WHEN PEOPLE ENCOUNTER babies, the first thing they usually comment on is the baby's appearance: the hair, the skin, how cute they are. Body-related comments, every one of them. In a way, this is understandable. Except for the crying and babbling, babies don't have much else going on in their lives.

Babies are cute. (Even the ones who look like little bald aliens.) So this focus on looks kind of makes sense. But what about when those babies grow older? When they become kids and teens and adults? Why does this focus on looks remain when there's so much else to us?

Why do other people comment on appearance?

Why do we still care?

How I felt about my appearance and fitting in

In middle school, I was desperately aware of how I looked compared with my friends. I was even more aware of how I looked compared with the people I *wanted* to be my friends. All the cool people had a certain pair of shoes (Doc Martens) and a certain brand of puffy jacket (Starter). They laughed with confidence and knew they were awesome. They were skinny and bubbly and played certain sports.

The popular kids made the rules, but even when I followed their rules, I still didn't feel good enough. Doc Martens hurt my feet. My parents said the jacket was too expensive. And when I tried to talk to the cool girls, my mind whirled like a fan during a heat wave, always second-guessing myself and trying to think of what the right thing to say might be.

When I got to high school, it was even worse. My school had an annual Halloween dance for the senior class, and that year, my friends and I decided to dress as devils. We went shopping together and bought sparkly headbands and red shirts. But when my friends arrived at my house so we could take pictures together, I rushed to my room and started bawling because I thought I was the fattest. At that point in my life, I thought that was a bad thing.

My freshman year of college, I compared myself with my two roommates the second we all met for the first time. Again, I concluded that I was the biggest.

But why did it even matter? I was in college to learn and to grow, not to be the thinnest person in the room.

It *did* matter, though, to me. At that time, it mattered to be seen as pretty and thin—and acceptable. I've always had a desire to fit in. Lots of people want this same thing. For many people, fitting in with certain groups is how we find a place in the world. It's how we make friends. We "fit in" with people who have the same interests, who play the same sports, who like the same TV shows. We form peer groups, which help us navigate the world. These groups help us not feel so alone.

It's okay to be different

Here's the thing, though: We can have things in common with people while still keeping the things that make us unique. Friend groups don't have to be alike in every way. You don't have to conform. Rather than making us feel separate and alone, our differences can set us apart *in a good way*. They can be the last piece that completes the friendship puzzle. All the pieces are different, but they're all crucial.

We *all* have differences, whether it's our body shape or skin color or something else. Some people are neurodivergent and interpret and interact with the world differently. Some people have chronic illnesses that they must manage on a daily basis. Some people are disabled and have to deal with an ableist world.

My body is part of who I am. It's not all of who I am, though.

It may not feel like it, but your body isn't what makes you special. If you gain or lose weight, that doesn't change who you really are.

You'll still be you, just in different clothes. You, with more or less sewn-together fabric covering you. You, in different wrapping paper.

Size doesn't sound so significant when you put it that way, does it? Everyone's wrapping paper is different. Everyone's insides are different, too. Depending on our backgrounds and particular circumstances, we all face unique challenges in our journeys to body acceptance.

It is so important—and so hard—to realize that everyone's healthy weight is going to be different.

That we all have different bodies.

That all of our bodies are worthwhile.

That we are more than our bodies. Our bodies are our shells. They cover what's inside of us. And what is inside of us is so, so wonderful. Focusing on what's "wrong" with our outsides only makes us neglect and forget to nurture all the good on our insides.

How size and appearance obsession can hurt us

Naomi Wolf's *The Beauty Myth*, written in 1991 yet still sadly relevant today, talks about how society continuously pushes women and girls toward creating and crafting an image of beauty and thinness.

The quest for some sort of perfect beauty is a distraction; Wolf talks about how women obsessed with their physical beauty can't also concentrate on their strength and their goals. They can be so focused on becoming the "ideal" that they are not focused on their careers or their causes, their interests or their passions.

In her introduction to the updated 2002 edition of the book, Wolf added a note that men also suffer from this "beauty myth."[78] Men have cosmetic surgery. Magazines are focused on male fitness and health. Men get eating disorders, too. And though Wolf doesn't mention nonbinary people, they—of course—can also be harmed by the beauty myth.

A study by the Centers for Disease Control and Prevention and the Los Angeles Unified School District found that boys are almost as likely as girls to purge or use laxatives. Similar results were found in other major cities across the United States.[79]

Sam J. Miller, author of the young adult novel *The Art of Starving*, suffered from depression and an undiagnosed eating disorder when he was younger.[80] Miller, who is gay, grew up in a homophobic small town and, as a result, suffered from a lot of self-hatred.

"I figured everyone would hate me if they knew my truth—even my parents, with whom I had a fantastic relationship. Even my teachers, who cared about and supported me. The self-harm I was engaged in through restrictive eating was just one more facet of that toxic swamp of internalized hate. And it literally didn't occur to me until years later that what I had was an eating disorder."

For a long time no one recognized his disorder, even though something was visibly wrong. Even after he went to the emergency room for stomach pains in the middle of the night. "People around me could see my damage, but they didn't know the extent or nature of it."

Miller doesn't know if he wasn't diagnosed because he was male, but it is a possibility. Eating disorders often look different in men and masculine people than they do in women and feminine people.

"Boys don't care about the thigh gap or the size of their buttocks," said Andrew Walen, founder of the Body Image Therapy Center and board president of the National Association for Males with Eating Disorders. "It's often about the waist up. It's a different presentation."[81]

Boys might suffer differently, but boys still suffer.

"The traditional statistic is that 10 percent of males

identify as eating disorder treatment seekers," Walen said. "But males are probably underreporting by 300 percent. The real number is probably a quarter to a third of all sufferers."

In 2007, a study by Harvard Medical School found that men made up about 25 percent of the study participants with anorexia or bulimia and close to *40 percent* of the participants who reported binge eating.[82] And a 2018 national assessment of thirteen-to-twenty-four-year-old queer youth in the United States found that 39% of transgender male youth had been diagnosed with an eating disorder, and 31% of cisgender (not trans) queer male youth had been diagnosed with eating disorders.[83]

Males and masculine people get eating disorders for any number of reasons, just as females and feminine people do. Often, the cause could be puberty or late development. Boys develop at different rates, leading to body differences between those who have been through puberty and those who haven't. Eating disorders often start as a result of bullying or peer pressure during adolescence, Walen said, when some boys may be "chubbier" than others.

"The media influences what is considered attractive," he said. "Which means there's no body fat. Guys are muscular. And this can't be realistically achieved without excessive exercise or steroids."

While many men and boys struggle with wanting to

develop more muscle, others strive to become as thin as possible. In 2018, Olympic figure skater Adam Rippon spoke to the *New York Times* about his previously restrictive eating habits, when he felt pressured to present a lean figure on the ice and reduce the appearance of his muscular thighs and buttocks.[84]

Regardless of *how* you think you must look, the beauty myth ends up controlling you—making you feel like you have to be perfect above all else. When we feel bad about ourselves, we will go on a diet. When we feel bad about ourselves, we will buy companies' products. We will buy special foods and gym memberships and pills. We'll buy whatever promises to make us feel or look better. It's a very persuasive way to get people to spend money.

The beauty myth turns us into an army of zombies, all obsessed with the same thing, even if we pursue it in different ways. Zombies don't smile. Zombies don't have the joy that we need to recover.

That's why we need to find our own definition of joy. By thinking about who we really want to be and what we want to achieve. By joining new groups and interacting with new people. By trying an activity that we were maybe too scared to try before—or picking up an old pastime that we let drift away.

This is our way of outrunning the zombies at our back. Not by being the best at "our bodies," but by realizing that so much else is out there to work for.

Find what you're good at and what you like to do

One thing that helped me discover who I was on the inside was to make one list of things that I was good at, and another of things that I liked to do. This is a distinction that a lot of people don't make: You don't have to be *good* at something to do it. There are no prerequisites to having fun. You don't have to stop an activity because you didn't make the team or haven't won any awards or people laugh at you. It's not *their* joy that matters. It's yours.

You can play the guitar without ever appearing on stage with a rock band. You can draw a picture of a dog that looks more like a horse and then stick it in your bottom drawer for no one to see ever—or you can display it. You can do things for the joy of it, because the simple act of liking them makes you *you*.

Here are some things that I really liked to do when I was younger:

- Swim
- Write short stories
- Sing
- Watch TV
- Play piano
- Ride my bike

I swam in high school, but I never made it to the Olympics. I sing in the car, but I never recorded an album. I still watch TV. I still ride my bike. I still (very rustily) bang out a few songs when I encounter a piano. I am a writer, but I would have kept writing even without this book.

Remember, you don't have to be good at everything

I'm not the best at everything, but for a long time I thought I had to be. And because I wasn't the best at my hobbies, I decided that I should make myself the best at something else.

So I became the best at my eating disorder. I became the best—but in the process I became something other than myself.

I became my body. Wanting to look like everyone else morphed me into someone completely unrecognizable, someone who was never satisfied. I always wanted to look better than everyone else. But above all, I always wanted to look better than "me." I was always a work in progress, someone I always had to improve, someone I always had to criticize.

I couldn't just *be*. I couldn't just *live*.

I was a good friend. I wanted to be a teacher and a writer. I loved going out for ice cream and seeing movies. I loved learning and laughing. None of that mattered anymore, though.

That should have mattered. That did matter.

Your life matters, too. Your body is important, of course. You live in it, and it's always working to keep you alive.

Our bodies work without our obsessing over them non-stop, though. Without letting those obsessions take over our lives and replace our interests.

Once you're no longer trapped inside your eating disorder, diet, food, and body obsession become boring. It becomes way more interesting to talk about things we've learned or how hard we've worked to achieve goals. Real goals, like making a sports team or making a new friend.

I can talk about that stuff for hours.

Your body? I'll get bored pretty fast. It's your outside. It's your skin.

Let's see your guts.

EXERCISE: THE THINGS YOU LIKE DOING

Make a list of things you enjoy doing.

Then think about your list. Have you stopped doing any of these enjoyable activities because you're not good at them? Or because you think you can't take part in them because of the way you look? What would it be like to do things you enjoy without worrying about being judged? What would you do if you knew that no one was rating your abilities or your body? What would your life be like then?

CHAPTER 17
Impostor Syndrome and Perfectionism

It's okay to feel bad and it's okay to be imperfect

DIFFERENT PEOPLE EXPERIENCE recovery in different ways. Just as our bodies are all unique, so are our personality traits. I am a perfectionist. I am an overachiever. That sounds awesome, right? Who wouldn't want to be perfect all the time?

Well, that's the thing. I'm *not* perfect all the time. *Nobody* can be perfect all the time. So I basically had a stream of unreachable goals that I was forever striving for. And when I didn't do things quite up to my standards, I yelled at myself. I called myself names, hoping to motivate myself to do better. Then I felt awful, which perpetuated the entire cycle.

(You know that term "a vicious cycle"? It really is vicious.)

On the outside, I probably looked as if I was totally in control. But on the inside, I felt like a fake, someone who had to work a million times harder than everyone else to have it all together. I felt like an impostor, the one fraud in a crowd full of people who knew exactly how to handle life.

What is impostor syndrome?

This kind of thing actually happens to so many people that there's a name for it: impostor syndrome. Impostor syndrome is what happens to high-achieving people who never truly feel as if they have "earned" their accomplishments or "deserve" the praise that comes their way. They feel as if they're just pretending or that they'll be exposed any minute.

If you have impostor syndrome, you're not alone!

Lots of famous people have impostor syndrome. Even after excelling for years, the following people, noted in various fields, still doubted that they deserved all their applause and compliments:

- Former First Lady Michelle Obama and Supreme Court Justice Sonia Sotomayor have both admitted that they felt like frauds at times.[85]

- So has award-winning actress Kate Winslet: "Sometimes I wake up in the morning before going off to a shoot, and I think, I can't do this; I'm a fraud."[86]
- Actress-comedian Tina Fey has talked about that feeling of "I'm a fraud! Oh God, they're onto me! I'm a fraud!"[87]
- And would you ever guess that Meryl Streep, perhaps the best actress of all time, said this? "You think, 'Why would anyone want to see me again in a movie? And I don't know how to act anyway, so why am I doing this?'"[88]
- Michael Uslan, the producer of the Batman movies, has said that he still feels like he doesn't belong on a movie set: "I still have this background feeling that one of the security guards might come and throw me out."[89]

For many, perfectionism can lead to eating disorders

When I was sick, I struggled with a mix of ambition and anxiety. I wanted to be perfect, but I didn't know if I could ever be good enough to get there. And when I moved closer to perfectionism, I always moved the bar higher. *Perfectionism*—not Ed, that voice I talk about in chapter eleven—was my demon. To be more precise, my perfectionism *led* to Ed. For me to truly vanquish my eating disorder, I had to deal with its root causes. It wasn't enough to simply separate out the messages it was sending me and ignore them.

Because when I did that, they kept coming. The noise always came back. Ed always crept back along my street and knocked at my door, like some overaggressive paparazzi photographer. I didn't know how to deal with him because I didn't know how to deal with *me*.

Ed was me. I was Ed. Ed arose from my unique personality traits. Ed was my way of dealing with the feelings that my impostor syndrome and perfectionism caused. That means that I had to confront and look at my personality in a different way before I truly recovered.

Instead of being perfect at losing weight, could I do really well at following my meal plan? At being honest? At kicking butt at this recovery thing? Could I see eating and rest, rather than appearance and grades, as victories?

Instead of believing that my victories were flukes, could I remember the steps I took along the way to achieve those goals and applaud myself for taking them?

Also, hardest of all, could I remember that no one is perfect? Can you?

How you can recover while dealing with perfectionism

In the end, I needed to realize how perfectionism in *any* form was harming me. I needed therapy to realize that I didn't have to be perfect. That my flaws don't make me a bad person.

I may be a little bit selfish, and I may be a little bit lazy at times. I have a tendency to not answer texts right away, and I am the worst at doing accents. I get random pimples on my chest every few months, and I get annoyed when people chew gum too loudly.

I have more flaws than those. I have tons of flaws. They might be annoying. They might be things that I have to work on, or things that I have to accept. But they're still part of me. Having them doesn't mean I have to torture myself for not being perfect.

Every single person has flaws. Everyone! Even the stunningly gorgeous supermodel marching down the runway or the toned quarterback who makes it to the Super Bowl every single year. Even the kid in your class who always has the newest thing. They all have flaws. They might *pretend* they don't, but they're there, somewhere, I promise.

Perfectionism makes us feel bad about ourselves, even though we're all flawed. We're all the same in that way. It wasn't until I realized this, until I made myself sit with my mistakes and forced myself not to apologize for being "wrong," that I started to realize that people wouldn't get angry at me if I wasn't perfect.

Eventually, *I* didn't get angry at myself for not being perfect. Because I was pretty cool the way I was. I'm pretty cool the way I *am*.

Finding yourself isn't simply about separating out Ed. It's about so much more. Let's dive into the "so much more" so you can *become* so much more.

EXERCISE: TURNING YOUR WEAKNESSES INTO STRENGTHS

Identify a personality trait of yours that may contribute to your eating disorder. Write down some of the ways this trait makes you engage in disordered eating, excessive exercise, or another harmful coping mechanism. What are some ways you can twist the characteristic around to make it work *for* you and your recovery?

CHAPTER 18

Learning How Exercise Can Be Harmful in a World Where Movement Is a Virtue

Exercise can be bad for you

WHEN I HAD an eating disorder, I exercised a lot. I'm not going to tell you what I did, even though I'm sure you want to know.

You are not wondering this, though. Your eating disorder is. It's wondering what actions I took, how hard I worked myself, and how sick I got. You might want to compare yourself with me, to prove how sick you are or to justify losing more weight.

I made those justifications, too.

When I was at the gym, I used to look at the machines of the people next to me to see how far and how fast they were running. I used to race them and feel superior when they stared at me with awe. (At least that's what I thought at the time. They were more likely staring at me with concern.)

I compared myself because those comparisons made it easier for my eating disorder to stay in my life. (And by that I mean take *over* my life.) I also compared myself because comparison is so easy to do with exercise.

Exercise addiction has, fortunately, started to be acknowledged as a legitimate part of an eating disorder, but many people still don't understand how exercise—something considered incredibly healthy—can be such a danger.

Often, it is the *lack* of exercise that is viewed as a danger instead. Lack of exercise *can be* a concern for many. People don't move as much as they used to, especially now that schools are cutting recess and gym class. But what is exercise, really? Exercise doesn't have to be running on a track or lifting weights. Exercise can be taking a walk or playing soccer or catch. Exercise can be a school dance. Exercise can be casual instead of structured and measured.

So exercise is good, right?

But what about when it's not?

Sports and possibly harmful messages about exercise

Lots of kids play sports. You might play soccer with your friends or on a team. You might take ballet lessons casually or do gymnastics before and after school. You might swim or run. That's exercise, whether you're competing at a high level or hanging out with your friends.

Ideally, you will listen to your body and rest when you're hurt. If you're on a structured team, your coach will make sure you take breaks, hydrate, and stay fueled.

The best coaches will do all of these things. The best coaches will know that you are not yet fully grown and that too much activity without the proper amount of rest or fuel will hurt you. It will hurt your body and your future.

Some coaches might ignore this, though. Some might encourage you to lose weight fast so that you can supposedly be more competitive. Wrestling coaches may look the other way when their athletes make a lower weight class or build muscle using unhealthy methods.

Exercise may be part of your life, but it's not your *entire* life. You were not put here on this earth to move or lift nonstop. Even if you love your sport, even if you think you might be able to make the Olympics someday, even if you're willing to sacrifice so many other things for exercise—it is still not your entire life.

But if we're bullied and think that our bodies aren't good enough, we may ignore the other important parts of ourselves. Or if we're praised and think that our bodies are the only things going for us, exercise and calories and body fat percentage may become our whole lives. The "ideal" body for a certain sport might taunt us, and the fact that our bodies will probably never achieve this ideal might torture us.

In the end, it's all about balance. We can work hard and train hard. But we also have to refuel and rest. We also have to accept the body and the limits that we have.

Balance can be hard, but a balanced life is important to happiness.

Learn what's healthiest for you despite bad influences

All too often, we hear messages that we need to tip that balance. To always watch what we eat. To always move. To exercise. To fit into a certain box that others expect us to inhabit.

Your parent might go to the gym and weigh themselves every day.

Your sibling might always be on a diet.

You might get teased because you're heavier than all your friends.

You might have started puberty early and look different from your peers.

Your lunch companions might always eat salads.

Your friend might run a certain amount every day.

You don't have to do any of these things, though. Other people are not better than you because they eat "better" or exercise more. They're different! (In fact, they might even be miserable, even though society might see them as amazing or virtuous or dedicated.)

Exercise is glorified and encouraged, and you're supposed to glorify it, too.

Some people might look at you strangely for sitting things out or behaving differently. But as cheesy as it sounds, the people who matter won't criticize you for changing. They won't mind that you do different things or that your body may be different. They'll be glad that you're happy and you're not hurting yourself with too much exercise.

In the end, it's *you* who matters. Your health and happiness matter, and the people who love you will know that and support you.

You need to love you, too. It's hard. Learning to love myself and my body was the hardest thing I've ever done. I'm still learning how to do it.

But the reward for all that hard work is that now I can allow myself to rest. I can let my body relax and repair itself, do what it wants, and have what it desires. Movement isn't a virtue in my life.

Love is.

EXERCISE (HAH! SEE WHAT I DID THERE?): WHY YOU EXERCISE

If you exercise, make a list of the reasons why. Then list how you feel when you are exercising. Are you happy? Unhappy? Tired? Do you wish you could take a day off?

Write about what you think would happen if you let your body do what it wanted, whether that means rest or an entirely different type of movement altogether. Are your fears realistic? If you're feeling brave, try to do what your body wants and see how you really *do* feel.

CHAPTER 19

What Do You Really Want Out of Life?

What do you want to be when you grow up?

YOU'VE PROBABLY HEARD this question a million times. If you're tall, other people may assume you want to be a basketball player, even though every time you touch a ball, your feet trip over themselves and your limbs buckle.

If you're good at math, your teacher might tell you you'd make a great engineer or rocket scientist. If you always have your head in a book, your parents might think you'll grow up to be a writer. A teacher. A poet.

You may like these comments people make, especially if they're urging you along a path you think you may want for yourself. Their words may give you confidence. If you want to be a veterinarian, it's encouraging to hear people say that you're great with animals. It's a confirmation that you're on the right path, that you know yourself well, and that your future is bright and clear, on its way to coming true.

Do other people want you to be something else?

But what if people assume things about you that you *don't* want for yourself? What if they want something that you don't value in the slightest?

People may not actually tell you what they think you should do or be. Sometimes you *feel* it instead. Sometimes you get hints at these messages from others' behavior. From the comments they make or the way people tease you.

Sometimes, a particular event in your past might take root in you, leaving you with feelings of guilt for not being "enough."

Wherever this pressure comes from, it doesn't feel good. It often doesn't feel *right* to follow the wishes of others. That feeling of discomfort is sending you an important message: Regardless of what other people want you to be, you need to stay true to *yourself*, in whatever way you're able to.

In the end, no matter the situation, "being true to yourself" comes down to self-love. It's about finding a way to accept a part of yourself that you might dislike or to pursue goals and interests that others might not understand. It is being true to your real self, not your eating disorder self. Sometimes the eating disorder comes as a way to ease the discomfort you might be feeling. Because if you are pursuing dreams that are not your own, you will feel discomfort. If you have to tell people that you want to follow a different path, you might feel afraid. While the eating disorder might help with the discomfort, it will not help you pursue your true dreams.

I now understand that there was no real reason to hate myself. I was fine. I *am* fine. I am different from other people, but everyone's different. No one is the same. It sounds cliché to say this, but it really would be a boring world if everyone looked and acted the same, if everyone did the same things and had the same interests.

Of course, you don't *have* to know what you want to do with your life. You may have no set plans or lots of different ideas for your future. This is totally normal. If you are in a situation that makes it hard to dream about the future, please don't despair. Things will get better. Things can change. You have time, I promise.

Not everyone grows up to be a superstar, famous, or conventionally "successful." The world may make it seem as if some people—and some lives—are better than others, but we are all people. Even if some people have more privilege and others face more challenges.

We all deserve to dream. We all deserve to lead our *own* lives. And that life starts from within. *You* define that life. Your life belongs to *you*.

Sometimes you'll feel bad about yourself, and that's okay

Even though I consider myself recovered from my eating disorder, I still have moments when my self-esteem is pretty awful. I compare myself with my friends whose lives seem way better than mine on social media. I get angry at myself when I get in a fight with a loved one. I criticize my body when I see some gorgeous actress in an advertisement.

It happens to me, and it will happen to you. It happens to everyone, no matter *how* self-evolved and recovered and confident they may be. Doubt and comparison are part of being human. The important thing is to identify those thoughts before they take over your brain, before you let one jealous thought about one single quality of another person take over your life entirely.

What to do if you wish you could swap lives

A wise friend once told me that whenever I compared myself with someone else or envied something about a person's life, I should envision the following scenario:

Imagine that you can swap lives with someone else. But you can't just trade one quality for another. You can't simply borrow someone's height or smile. You can't take someone's sense of humor or muscles or love life. If you want someone else's life, you will have to take it all. You'll have to trade lives entirely.

Would you choose to swap lives? If you're jealous of something that someone has, would it be worth giving up *all of you* to take over that single enviable quality? You'd lose your family and your friends. You'd lose everything else that makes you you.

You are made up of *all* your qualities. You are strengths and flaws and hopes and dreams. Your dreams and goals may not align with what others expect for and from you, but this doesn't mean that you are wrong or on the wrong path.

Your goals and your interests don't have to align with the world's.

You are part of the world. Without you, there is a hole in the universe. Without your interests, there is a void. Empty space. Nothingness.

Without you, the world is diminished.

You are important. You are vital.

You belong, no matter who you are or what you want to do with your life. The universe wouldn't be complete without you.

EXERCISE: YOUR PERFECT DAY

If you didn't have to worry about judgment or fitting in, what would be your perfect day? What time would you wake up? What would you do first thing in the morning? Would you watch TV? Go outside? Be active? Relax? Who would you spend time with? How does thinking about this day make you feel? How would the day itself make you feel? What is one way you can make tomorrow be more like this one perfect day?

CHAPTER 20

Role Models and Media Literacy

Why do we look up to role models and celebrities?

WHEN I WAS in middle school and high school, I was really into celebrity gossip. I loved awards shows and movies and television.

I never became one of the celebrities I dreamed about, but fame wasn't what I really wanted anyway. What I really wanted was validation that I was okay. That I was good enough. That I was *as good as* these beautiful people everyone else admired so much.

You might not admire celebrities as I did. You might admire your older brother or your baseball coach. You might admire your aunt or your friend who always has it together. You might follow their actions as I tracked the paths of celebrities on the red carpet. You might want to be them.

Why?

Why do you want to be like them? What do they have that's better than what you have already? How are they somehow better than who you are?

Admiration vs. envy

These are the questions I still ask myself whenever I find myself admiring or envying someone else. Because there's a fine line between admiration and envy. I might admire some aspect of my friend's life—her great job, for example—while still not wanting it for myself. She might make a lot of money and thus be able to buy lots of clothes and go on lots of trips.

But (there's always a but) that friend may have to work twelve-hour days. She's never home. She's exhausted all the time. That kind of trade-off isn't worth it for me. I don't envy what she has; I just admire one aspect of her life.

Admiration makes me feel good for someone else: *Wow, how awesome! She must be so happy she got asked to the dance. It's so great he won that wrestling championship.*

Envy is the opposite side of that coin. It's the parallel dimension where up is down and everything gets twisted. Envy makes me think that my friend got asked to the dance because her body is better than mine. And if that's true, then it *also* must be true that *I* didn't get asked because I'm ugly and unlovable.

My admiration of celebrities would often turn into envy, reflecting back upon myself. If I admired some aspect of their fame or beauty or money that I didn't have, then I felt bad about myself because I would never be as wonderful or as perfect as they were.

Polished pictures make us buy things to feel better

Here's the thing: Role models are not as perfect as they seem. The pictures of people in magazines undergo massive amounts of airbrushing before they're printed and set before our eyes. Their pimples and blemishes are erased. Their cellulite is smoothed out. Inches are digitally carved off their waists and thighs. Sometimes their skin color is even changed. Magazines have gone as far as lightening the skin of black celebrities such as Beyoncé and Kerry Washington.[90]

What does it mean when the appearances of these "beautiful people" are modified to be closer to a specific beauty standard (usually white, cis, able-bodied, and thin)? What does it do to people who rarely see their skin color represented in the media?

In her article "4 Ways Our Socially Accepted Beauty Ideals

Are Racist," Rachel Kuo talks about how she "started to realize that my discomfort around my looks and my body exist because these images I saw every day didn't allow room for multiple ways of looking and being. As women of color, we should be able to feel our own beauty on our own terms."[91]

Beauty norms are usually defined by the culture, whether stated directly by the people around us or by media like movies, television, books, and advertisements.

So what happens when disabled people don't see people like themselves on-screen?

What happens when those who are fat aren't represented?

What happens when people of color don't appear on magazines or book covers as often as white people?

What does it mean when every image we see has been digitally modified and professionally lit? When no one is allowed to be their true, natural selves?

Unfortunately, "true" and "natural" are not shown very often in the media. And even if we *know* these fake images are altered, we see them so much that we start to believe our eyes more than our brains. Then, because of these delusions, we feel bad about ourselves.

Celebrity role models may *look* "perfect" on the screen or on paper, but they're not. They have imperfections, too. We just can't see their "flaws" because they're covered up.

Dove's Campaign for Real Beauty video shows just how much makeup and digital post-production work goes into models' photos.[92]

(Spoiler alert: It's a lot.)

It is someone's *job* to make these models into an "ideal." It is *many* people's jobs, actually. Their job is to fool you into wanting to look like these stars.

Because then you'll feel bad about yourself. And when you feel bad about yourself, you'll buy something from someone. The goal is to get you or your parents to buy clothes, makeup, a training session, a movie ticket—whatever they're selling.

Celebrities exercise and diet as if it's *their* job—because it *is* their job. It's their job to take on this "ideal" form, and they devote way more time to it than the average person can. Celebrities get paid for it, though. And they have help: nutritionists and personal trainers and even people to coach them on what to say in interviews to sound smooth and confident and witty.

Beauty bloggers on Instagram especially undergo these transformations. They know all the tricks to make themselves look a certain way: contouring and shading and filters. It's the *results* of these tricks that you see. Image is a job for them—but that image is the result of a lot of time, effort, and money.

Of course, if you are into makeup, that's wonderful. Makeup is a hobby for many people and wearing it can be empowering. But for others, the need to wear lipstick and blush and eyeliner is another result of society's message that we must conform to a certain flawless image. And the drive to meet those standards can take a lot of work, work that will take you away from your true interests.

Some countries have taken steps to ban underweight models so they do not end up "inspiring" those who watch them on the runways. Many models have eating disorders to try to fit into their field's impossible ideals, but as of May 2017, France requires a doctor to certify every model's health.[93] This is a step—a required step with punishments and fines—that can hopefully lead to these models getting the eating disorder recovery support they need.

But looking at models isn't the only problem. For some, models are only images on paper. They aren't truly "real." For many people, the real problem is not the images of strangers in the media, but the images of friends on social media. When you see classmates and peers having fun without you or when you see them through the filtered lens of a certain app, it can make you feel bad. But you don't know what's going on beyond the frame. You don't know the whole story of why you weren't invited to a specific get-together. You don't know what's really behind the filter.

What is media literacy?

We need to train ourselves to look at the images and messages we're getting from the media and analyze them. To realize that someone is trying to sell us something. This type of analysis, or dissection of the images presented to us, is called media literacy.

Media literacy can be hard.

Because we're so used to these pictures of perfection.

Because we've already accepted that there won't be images of "people like me" out there.

Because some part of us may want them to be real.

Because if these images are real, maybe *we* can look like that, too, someday, and maybe the product they're advertising will help. Right?

Wrong.

That's why I admire people who defy conventional beauty standards, who focus on their inner strengths instead of constantly adorning themselves. Being a celebrity isn't a bad thing, after all. Being pretty or admirable in whatever way isn't bad. I just like to go deeper now, to stop and think about what's *beneath* the beauty or the filter. When I consider what qualities I truly admire and want to emulate—whether it's confidence, kindness, or bravery—then I can stop that cycle of self-abuse before it starts.

Instead of feeling bad about what I'm not, now I think about what I want to be. I think about how I can possibly cultivate other positive traits in my own life.

I don't have to hate myself. I don't have to think I'm unlovable. Because those wonderful qualities that I look up to in other people—I can often find them in myself, too. And if not, I can work toward them.

EXERCISE: WHO DO YOU ADMIRE?

Make a list of people you look up to. Why do you admire them? Is it because of their appearance? What are some nonbeauty and lifestyle-based qualities that you aspire to? Who has those qualities? How can you cultivate those qualities in yourself?

CHAPTER 21

Where Did This Come From?
Considering the Role of Family

How do family and environment factor into eating disorders?

SOMETIMES THE PLACE you live and your particular family dynamics can affect your eating disorder.

Biology student Michelle, who is Filipino American, said, "Food, especially traditional Filipino food, has always been a large part of my life. So much of the colorful culture of the Philippines centers around Filipino cuisine, and for as long as I can remember, so have my family's gatherings with our loved ones and friends.

"But alongside these joyful memories of food are ingrained lessons that food is something to be feared. From a very young age, I was inundated with the 'feminine' values of traditional Filipino culture, which included being 'thin,' so men will think that you are beautiful, and so that you will find a husband. This message ran directly counter to the fatty, flavorful textures that are so synonymous with Filipino food, and so as a child, I struggled to find the right balance between indulging in a cultural tradition and conforming to the standards expected of me by the same heritage."[94]

Living in an insular, homogenous Midwestern community also contributed to some of Michelle's discomfort with food and her body. "I was being brought up in a community where white, Western beauty was the paradigm," she explained. "I grew up believing that I could never be beautiful because I was not white—not of my own invention, but because this was what my peers believed."

These pressures and beliefs from your extended family or community can affect how you see yourself. Messages from parents can often have a more significant effect. Sometimes, even with parents who try to understand, it can be hard to express what you're going through.

"My parents have always been broadly supportive of my mental and physical health," Michelle said, "but because of the cultural context they grew up in, they don't really know how to interact with mental health, and as a result, the topic never really comes up with them. Most of the time this is fine, since I'm always away at college and see them so infrequently, but sometimes it's frustrating when food-induced anxiety makes me irritable and snippy with them and I feel like I can't explain why I'm acting that way or that I don't mean to be."

It's normal to have to think through your interactions with your family as you recover, and to struggle to find the best way to express yourself and communicate your needs.

It's also normal for members of your support network to struggle to understand your eating disorder.

You might complain about your parents. I did. They may have contributed to your feelings of low self-esteem. They may *still* do things that make you feel as if you have to be different from who you are. They may be on diets themselves.

When I was sick, I got mad at my parents a lot. I remembered the comments they had made about my body. I thought about the pressure I felt to never express my negative emotions.

I talked in therapy about ways in which my family "made recovery harder." After I left my residential treatment program, I actually lived with my aunt for a while. Some part of me thought that separating myself from the environment where I'd developed my eating disorder would cure me.

Nothing changed, though. Because my family *wasn't* the root cause of my eating disorder. My parents may have acted in ways that triggered my anxiety or caused me to feel bad about myself, but they didn't mean to hurt me. My eating disorder made me interpret their comments in certain ways. My eating disorder made me choose to exercise and restrict my food in response.

My family was *one* factor in the development—not *the* cause—of my anorexia.

Your family may be a factor in your disordered eating or body image issues. Your friends may be a factor. Your socio-economic background may be a factor. Genetics and biology are also a factor—a 2017 study done by lead researcher Cynthia Bulik at the UNC School of Medicine found that there are specific genetic variations in those who suffer from anorexia nervosa. Bulik also found that other diseases, such as schizophrenia, type 1 diabetes, and certain autoimmune disorders, were caused by the same genes.[95]

It all mixes together. Unfortunately, it's impossible to identify that one moment in time when our eating disorder was born. It's impossible to find that one person or situation that caused it all.

The only thing we can do is work on our own behavior—on our own responses to the people and situations that trigger us in our daily lives.

As I mentioned, my parents didn't mean to pressure me to be perfect. But regardless of their motives, I did get that message. I *was* affected. It took me a long time—I still struggle with it today—to realize that I am allowed to speak up. I am allowed to tell people how they are affecting me.

This doesn't mean that I am blaming them. It simply means that I am declaring to the world that my feelings are just as valid as those of my loved ones.

When family makes your disordered eating worse

In life, and especially in recovery, others can be unaware of how things they say and do affect you. They may not understand that your brain may interpret the comment "You look so healthy!" as "You've failed!" They don't know that staring at you while you eat might make you fall back on disordered eating.

But even if people don't understand what they're doing, they can still hurt you through their words or actions or implicit messages. Mental harm can be just as painful—and have just as dangerous consequences—as physical harm. You can and should speak up to protect your recovery. If you don't feel comfortable doing it in the moment, this is a great scenario to discuss with a therapist or a trusted friend. You could role-play how to speak up in the future, or even hold a family meeting with a mediator present.

My parents *did* contribute to my eating disorder. They never directly told me I wasn't good enough, but they did constantly praise my achievements. This sounds silly to complain about, but this constant positive feedback loop actually had a negative effect, as I started to internalize this always-achieving identity. When I struggled, it was hard for me to admit my "failures," because I was often met with a motivational speech:

"Get over it and keep going. I know you can do it."

"The true measure of success is not giving up."

"Crying never solved anything."

I didn't want a pep talk, though. I wanted to be heard. I wanted permission to feel. Because feeling sad is okay. Getting angry is okay. Expressing yourself is more than okay.

How to talk to your family about their effect on your disordered eating

My family's words weren't intentionally cruel, but they didn't acknowledge the other part of me: the part that wasn't perfect. The part that should have been told that struggle is okay. That allowing oneself time to grieve and cry and mourn is, in fact, part of the healing process. It's part of the growing process.

This is something I speak up about now:

"I'm feeling sad and that's okay."

"Right now, I need someone to listen, not to solve my problem."

"I messed up. Oh, well."

Parents are hard, whether they're in your life or not. Whether they're supportive or absent, divorced or married. Many want to help you feel good about yourself and your body, while some won't care. Some will insult you. Some will criticize you. Some won't have time for you.

This is why it's so important to advocate for yourself throughout recovery and to seek out the people who can help you the most. If your parents or caregivers are not healthy supports for you, try to find friends, a teacher, a counselor, or a support group that can help. There are people out there to talk to and people who can help. It may take time, but there are ears out there to listen.

Bonding, "fat talk," and when family members feel bad about their own appearance

In many families, parents can reinforce the appearance ideals that they grew up with and believe themselves. Some people I talked to while writing this book had mothers who went on diets with them and taught them "purging tricks." Children may see their parents—particularly mothers—weighing themselves every morning or complaining about how fat they are. They talk about the body parts they want to slim and the pounds they want to lose.

Marie Southard Ospina, a Colombian American freelance journalist and fat positive activist, talked to me about the clash—and the similarities—between her Colombian family's beauty ideals and other beauty ideals.[96]

"I realized pretty early on into my teens that whenever I lost weight, I also lost my curves. This would be greeted by comments like 'Now you look like a boy' by the same relatives who'd previously encouraged the weight loss.

"But if I stayed fat, or even just a little bit chubby, I felt out of place in both cultures. I felt like that because I was treated as such. Honestly, trying to appease two cultural ideals of beauty was exhausting—and no one was ever 'happy' with the way I looked regardless of my size."

As is the case for most of us, Southard Ospina's body didn't perfectly match the external beauty standards she felt pressured to meet.

Trying to meet *any* standard imposed on you takes effort. It takes mental energy and physical energy. It's emotionally draining because it makes people see their bodies as the problem.

The truth is that these *standards* are the problem.

"You need to remember that the problem is *not* your body," Southard Ospina said. "The problem is the way people respond to your body. You don't need to lose weight, or go on a crash diet, or strive to be like the people you see in glossy magazines. It might seem impossible now, but one day you'll meet people who get it. You'll realize that 'fat' doesn't have to be an insult. It doesn't have to be a death sentence. It doesn't have to mean that you'll always be unhappy. It's just a body type. A beautiful, supercool body type, for a beautiful, supercool person. The world is full of amazing fat people living their lives freely. You just need to find them—and let them guide you instead. My philosophy is simple, I suppose: Your body (no matter its shape, size, race, abilities, gender identity, etc.) is not a mistake."

But it can be hard to be at peace with your body, especially when others often expect—and even encourage—you *not* to be.

While people of any gender can be harmed by this type of negative body talk, these messages may particularly harm females and feminine people. In fact, women often bond through this "fat talk," where the main topic of conversation is weight/dieting/their own or others' appearances.

Person One: "I look so fat!"

Person Two: "No, I look so fat! You look great!"

This type of talk makes us feel bad about ourselves. It makes us compare. It reinforces the pressure to look a certain way. And it also establishes weight and appearance as the most important thing in the world.

Males and masculine individuals reinforce standards of masculinity in similar ways. Parents may encourage their children who are assigned male at birth to be tough, or they may scorn them for acting effeminate. Parents might push children who are assigned male at birth into activities that are seen as masculine, like football, while they might frown upon a child who was assigned female *wanting* to play.

Some caregivers refuse to dress children who are assigned male at birth in pink.

Not every family does this. Not everybody engages in negative talk about their own bodies. Not everybody enforces gender roles and body standards.

Some families do, though.

Some families have *other* pressures and expectations.

Your family may not know the right way to help you right now. If you can, try to find a family therapist who can meet with all the members of your family at the same time. Disordered eating is something that can affect the entire dynamic of a household.

When I was in recovery, my parents used to watch me prepare food and urge me to put more on my plate. They hid the scale so I couldn't weigh myself. They told me I was too skinny all the time.

I felt smothered when my parents acted like the food police. I felt anxious, which made me focus on my body even more, which led me to restrict my food intake and ultimately relapse. Then the whole attempt to recover started all over again.

My parents didn't mean to do anything wrong. Neither did I. We were simply trying to communicate with each other in our own ways, and things fell apart in the translation.

The translation is the tricky part. Just as you do with Ed, you need to have a dialogue with your parents when they say things that are unhelpful. You may need to have similar conversations with your grandparents. With your brothers and sisters and your friends. Maybe even with your teachers and coaches. You will have to communicate what you need throughout your entire struggle to recover from disordered eating. It will be hard, but you can do it, especially if you think about what you want to say beforehand. If you consider what bothers you about their behavior and what others can do to change.

Don't blame them.

Don't tell them everything is their fault. It probably isn't. But part of it may be. And to move on, you and they may both have to learn to accept that. If there are no issues of trauma or abuse, you can put what happened in the past.

Now is the time to focus on how *you*—and on how *others*—can change.

Expressing yourself with "I feel when" statements

One script that helped me when I was recovering was the "I feel when" statement:

"I feel _____ when you _____ because _____."

This statement can be adapted to any number of situations:

- Parents who criticize your body and comment that you need to lose weight
- Parents who hover and act like the food police, taking control of your eating
- Parents who are too busy to notice that you are struggling
- Parents who are on diets and are obsessed with their food

Here are some examples of how to use this script:

- "When you said that I shouldn't order that meal, I felt as if you didn't like the way I look. I'm trying hard to listen to what my body wants, and I'm really hungry right now."
- "When you didn't come home for dinner tonight as you promised, I felt abandoned. I'm really nervous about eating by myself still, and I'd love your support."
- "I feel self-conscious when you talk about how you don't like how your body looks and how many calories are in everything we eat. I'm trying to remove those words from my life, and it's harder to do when you act as if you value thinness over everything else."

- "It makes me nervous when you stare at me while I'm eating. I'm trying my best to follow my meal plan, and all this hovering makes me feel as if you don't trust me."
- "When you tell me I need to go to the gym more, I feel as if you don't think I'm good enough. I'm working really hard to get better at football, and I'd love for you to acknowledge that."

These scripts can be hard to plan. They can be hard to say. It can be even harder to deal with the reactions. Your family members may feel attacked. They may protest or deny. They may walk away or say something that hurts you even more.

But it's important for you to be able to stand up for yourself and your needs, even if you make someone you love upset or surprised.

Of course, this script will not work for every situation. Your caregivers may not react in the ways you want them to, especially at first. They may continue to say or do hurtful things. They may not respect your wishes.

NOTE: If you are in a dangerous situation at home, please seek out a trusted relative, a school guidance counselor, a friend, or a therapist to talk to instead. There are resources in the back of this book that can help you find a therapist.

EXERCISE: FAMILY ISSUES

What are some common issues you run into with your family members? Write down some of the things they say that hurt your feelings or make you feel anxious. Write your own script about what to say to them when they do something unhelpful for your journey to body acceptance.

EXERCISE: ENCOURAGING FRIENDS

Make a list of people you can turn to for reassurance when your family negatively affects you. Talk to these people when you need encouragement that it is okay to be who you are.

CHAPTER 22

Selfie Culture, Social Media, and Comparison

The pressure to look perfect

IN TODAY'S WORLD, your image is probably everywhere. You might bring your phone to a party and take pictures with your friends. Your parents might record your athletic event on their phones. You might take a selfie. Then you feel self-conscious about how you look and delete it.

You might make sure your good side is facing the camera and carefully cultivate the image you put out there so that you always look polished, happy, and in control of your life. You may *feel* sick or stressed or angry at the world, but in a picture you look good. In a picture, things can be okay.

It's not just kids and teenagers who feel this way. Adults do, too. When I'm updating my status or uploading pictures,

I often think about how I'm going to look to others. I take and retake pictures if I think my nose is scrunched up all weird or if I'm not smiling enough. When I write a status or a caption, I consider how my words are going to be received.

I think negative thoughts sometimes. I'm still critical of my body and my life, even years into recovery, even now that I respect my body. These thoughts are normal for everyone, whether people are struggling with body acceptance or they've never had a single negative thought about their bodies. (Although I highly doubt these alien creatures exist.) Human beings find fault with themselves. *You* will find fault with yourself, especially since you're still growing. Your body may be changing, and that can be a strange experience.

Growing up can be awkward and disorienting. Growing up involves change, especially in puberty. And when we change, we notice.

We examine ourselves, in the pictures we take and in the image we present.

It's okay to be imperfect

I still take awkward pictures as an adult, but not because I'm going through puberty. I take awkward pictures because I'm human. Because I burp and fart and hiccup and make silly expressions. There are days when I don't feel like smiling and someone takes my picture anyway. Days when I don't want to pretend that my life is the best thing ever.

Before, when I hated myself and thought I didn't deserve happiness, I would have taken these feelings and looked at these unflattering photos and believed that they were confirmation of my unworthiness. Confirmation that I'd never be as attractive as I wanted to be. Confirmation that the new exercise regimen I'd started was the best idea ever.

I didn't stop to consider the fact that everyone has bad days. Even the perfect people on social media have bad days.

They just know how to hide it.

If someone adds a filter to a photograph or puts on some makeup, they can be completely transformed. If they write about how amazing their life is, people believe them.

A 2013 *New York Times* article "The Agony of Instagram" called this phenomenon "Instagram envy." It's when we look at pictures of our friends having fun without us or looking amazing, and feel as if we're missing out.

Instagram and other social media sites allow people to "idealize every moment." One Instagram user in the article noted, "You're searching through your feed and a picture will hit you. . . . It's just so perfect. You just think, 'I want that, I want that life.'"[97]

A 2016 study by the School of Psychology in Australia found that young people most often compare themselves with images on social media and that these comparisons make them think they are less attractive than what they see.[98] These comparisons make them think about dieting and exercising more. They affect their mood.

Social media has become a culture of comparison, and we always end up on the losing side. And for people struggling with disordered eating or self-esteem, the natural instinct is to "fix" their bodies or create a "perfect image" of their own.

Maybe we can do the same things as our awesome friends and these social media celebrities, we think. Maybe if we present *our* images in this same way, then the world will believe that *we're* magical and perfect, too.

Maybe *we* will believe it.

I think that's what it comes down to: this belief that if you present the "right" image, if you take the best photographs of yourself in the most flattering light and craft your words so your life looks amazing, then it has to eventually be that way, right?

It doesn't work that way, though. You can pretend for a really long time. You can probably pretend for your entire life, but it's going to be hard. It's going to hurt because instead of enjoying your life, you'll be too busy working to stuff yourself into someone else's life—just as you've been spending so much time trying to shrink yourself down into a different body.

When I started being honest about my flaws and my struggles, life became easier. I didn't have to spend all my energy on creating some perfect persona anymore; I could spend that energy on things I wanted to do instead.

The funny thing is that when I started admitting that my life wasn't perfect, people didn't care. Instead, they related. They shared their own struggles, and we became closer. They told me how their "fabulous" picture was just a snapshot in an otherwise imperfect life. We became real together.

You are you, and no picture or caption or status update is going to change that. Deep down, you know the truth. You know that the images you see online and the pictures people send you aren't always reality. You know that everyone has hard days and days when they feel unhappy with the way they look. You know that looking bad in a picture doesn't make you fat or ugly or wrong.

It makes you human.

Posting a filtered picture or pretending to be someone you're not isn't going to help you belong. Changing your body isn't going to help you belong.

Finding yourself is going to help you belong. *Being genuine* is going to help you belong. Realizing what your interests and talents are and who you truly have fun with is going to help you belong. When you spend so much time presenting a false image to the world, there's no time or energy left for you to focus on what's real.

There is a real you in there, a you without witty, planned-ahead banter, a you stripped bare of filters. *That* you admits when you're having a hard day and tells the world when you make a mistake. *That* you looks silly and weird and awkward sometimes.

That you is true.

I still think about how my body looks. I criticize it sometimes. I compare it. But those moments pass quickly. For the most part, I see myself, and I notice myself. I may comment on myself, but I don't hate myself. I appreciate my body for what it is and what it can do for me. I give myself compliments.

Then I go and live my life.

The funny thing is that *you* might seem that same way to others. You may be the person that *other* people measure themselves against.

So let them see the real you, not an illusion.

Let's be real. All of us.

EXERCISE: ALL THE GOOD THINGS

Make a list of all the awesome, fantastic, smile-worthy stuff that has happened to you in the past week. If you take pictures, make a note of all the photos in which something great happens.

Now, imagine what your "image" would be if someone only saw *these* pictures and heard about *these* high points in your life. Would that image be reality? Do you think others might compare themselves with *you*?

Remember that this same thing happens to you when *you're* viewing social media. Next time you're scrolling through someone's feed, try to fill in the blanks between the pictures and updates. Remember that *everyone's* life has its ups and downs.

PART FOUR

As You Recover

CHAPTER 23
Strengthening Relationships

When your eating disorder is more important than friends and family

WHEN I HAD an eating disorder, the most important thing in my life was keeping my eating disorder secret. Keeping it *mine*. Other people wanted to take it away from me. They said it was hurting me. They said I was sick. They didn't understand, though. They didn't know how my eating disorder made me feel less anxious. How it made me feel special.

They were wrong. They *had* to be wrong. They wouldn't listen. They wouldn't learn.

That's why I started pulling away from everyone who cared about me. It felt as if they were out to hurt me. It felt as if everything they did was an attack.

My mother wanted to make me eat more. My best

friends kept offering to share their food. My therapist told me to cut back on my exercise.

I thought they wanted to ruin my life.

I loved my family. I loved my friends. I liked my therapist. But in those moments, when these people confronted me, I truly felt as if the world was conspiring against me. I thought that people were jealous, that the world wanted to sabotage me by taking away the only thing I was good at.

Of course, it wasn't like that at all. My parents and my friends saw how sick I was. They could tell that I couldn't stop myself from exercising. They understood (even if they never *truly* understood) that I was stuck. That's why they were trying to help.

They really *were* trying to help.

What they didn't understand was that my brain made their actions seem like a betrayal.

When I was in the depths of my illness, I was good at hiding how sick I was. I was good at lying about what I ate (or didn't eat). I was good at looking at numbers on exercise machines and on shiny see-through scales.

You might be the same way. You may know exactly how to hide your behavior after meals or late at night. You might lie about what you're doing to change your body and relieve your anxiety. (You might even be lying to yourself in some ways.)

I was good at lying. So as I "learned" not to trust my

family and friends, they learned not to trust me. When I broke plans. When I yelled and cried. When they inevitably found out the truth. This is obviously not the basis for a good relationship. In fact, it can destroy relationships, which need honesty to grow and thrive.

Are you lying to hide your eating disorder or excessive exercise?

One of the biggest danger signs with an eating disorder is lying about your behavior. When I was sick, I lied to cover up what I did. If I told the truth, I wouldn't be able to do those things anymore. I *wanted* to do those things. Those things were my identity. What I needed to survive, to not feel anxiety and discomfort bubbling up inside me every second of every day.

I wanted to be sick more than I wanted other people in my life.

Right now, you might feel the same way. You might feel as if the world is conspiring against you. As if there's some big plan to take away the only thing that helps you feel better.

Disordered eating may make you feel better in the moment, but it hurts in the end

Your eating disorder and your obsession with your body may make you feel better in the moment. They may relieve your anxiety briefly. But in the end, an eating disorder leaves you all alone. In the end, it stops you from having a life. It stops you from having experiences and making memories.

Looking back on when I was really sick, I can't identify one truly happy memory. Of course I smiled and laughed and made jokes during those years, but I was never care-free. I never let myself live in the moment fully. Something else was always pulling at my brain—a worry, a calculation, a feeling of discomfort or unease. I wouldn't let myself be truly happy because I didn't *deserve* to relax and be free.

That's what I thought, at least.

Connecting to people you love will make you feel better

All my positive memories came from before I got sick, before counting calories and comparing bodies became as natural as breathing. Back when people and friends were better than isolation and silence:

- Spending family vacations on Cape Cod, walking through the town center and playing Wiffle ball on the beach with my family
- Singing random advertising jingles with my best friend in her front yard, then dissolving into giggles when cars drove by with their windows open
- Waking up early on Christmas and tip-toeing down the stairs with my younger brothers
- Celebrating my tenth birthday with a surprise party
- Going to the bookstore with my dad in the middle of a hurricane because I just *had* to have a book to read during the storm

None of my memories involve sitting at a lunch table with nothing in front of me. None of my memories feature me, alone, running away my pain.

My memories involve connection. They involve trust and laughter and love.

How many times have you laughed lately? Not a fake laugh. Not a laugh that you think people are expecting. Not a laugh where, in the back of your mind, you're wondering what the scale will say the next morning.

When I was sick, I rarely laughed. I was too busy thinking about how to hide my eating disorder.

Being sick isn't joyful; it's exhausting. It uses up a lot of brainpower and a lot of energy, energy that is way better used to connect with other people and with the world.

Reaching out to people again is scary—especially after you've deliberately rejected them in the past. They might reject *you*. They may be mad at you. They may not trust you. They may be so used to you canceling plans that they don't think to invite you anywhere anymore.

You may wonder what will happen if you *do* get rejected. Why spend energy on recovery if your friends won't be there for you when it's all over? If you're going to end up alone, why not stick with what's already working? Why not stay sick?

There are *lots* of reasons not to stay sick. We'll talk about them in the next section.

You can't have your eating disorder forever

Above all, you need to remember that staying sick with your eating disorder is not an option. As you recover and reach out to friends you've alienated, your friends *may* reject you. They may not forgive you for pushing them away when you were sick.

This happened to me. I lost friends, friends I had lied to and canceled plans on. They stayed mad. They didn't understand how my illness had caused me to withdraw. Some of them I don't talk to anymore. Some of them I'm friends with again, although the bond isn't the same. It will never be the same.

It stinks. There's no way to sugarcoat that. Losing friends stinks, especially when it's your "fault." (Even though I now know that I was sick and that my actions truly weren't my fault.) I've forgiven myself and have moved on, even though it still hurts to think about the changes in those relationships.

I kept most of my friends, though. I apologized, and they tried to forgive. I made an effort to seek *them* out instead of waiting for my friends to come find me. At first, we tried to do things that didn't involve food. We talked about happy times in the past and made new memories. We didn't mention my new body or the ways in which my behavior had changed.

It was awkward at first, but with time the awkwardness melted away. We remembered who we were and who we'd been before. If our friendship was a chain, some of the earlier links had rusted, but they didn't break, and we kept adding shiny new links—ones that held on tight.

Because *we* held on tight, even if we almost fell apart.

Making new friends

You may make new friends after your recovery, too, friends who fit better with the new and recovered version of you. Before, your friendships may have been abusive or unsupportive. Your friends may have teased you or encouraged you to diet. Those friendships were unhealthy. Those friendships hurt you.

As you recover, you will be different. Eventually, you will feel more confident. You will be closer to embracing who you truly are and what activities you truly enjoy doing. You'll be ready to find people you enjoy being with, people who accept you for who you are. People who raise you up instead of lowering you down.

Sometimes you won't find these friends right away. You may live in a community where people aren't accepting of you, for whatever reason. You may encounter resistance against who you are or who you are becoming. Though you may feel alone now, it gets better. Your people are out there. You may find them in a different grade or a different school. You may find them online. Your community *is* out there, ready to welcome you in.

Earning back the trust of the people you've hurt

Things will also change with your family as you move through the stages of recovery: If you've lied to them in the past, they may not trust you for a while. Family members or caregivers may look at you strangely every time you go to the bathroom. They may ogle your plate and suggest that you eat certain things. They may monitor your late-night activities or want to exercise with you, "just in case."

(They may be huge pains in the butt.)

Not being trusted is awful. I remember being so angry that everyone around me didn't believe I had recovered. I got so angry that sometimes the anger twisted and morphed, leading me to do something that wasn't healthy. Leading me to skip a meal because *Why shouldn't I? They expect me to mess up anyway.*

Of course, this made them watch me more. Which made *me* snap at them and avoid them and proclaim huffily, "I don't need you."

I did need them, though. You'll need people, too, whether it's your family or a close friend or a therapist or a support group. You'll need people to hold your hand as you tiptoe through recovery. And if those people have been in your life for a long time, they may be worried for a long time.

I had to keep reminding myself that my family's actions stemmed from concern. (Okay, my therapist told me to remind myself of that.) My loved ones were watching me so closely because they cared and wanted to make sure I recovered.

I tried to remember that when I did finally recover, they would act normally around me again. I would earn their trust back.

You can earn trust back, too. With each healthy decision you make, with each urge to binge or purge or restrict or overexercise that you resist, with every friend you text or invitation you accept, you are strengthening your relationships and your recovery.

You are doing it.

Your friends and family aren't the enemy for wanting to take your eating disorder away. Your eating disorder is the enemy. *It* is taking your life away. *It* is taking your happiness away.

Life won't be 100 percent wonderful once you recover. Every future memory of yours will not be positive. That's okay. We're not looking for perfection here. We're not aiming for a life that's only sunshine and blue skies.

You may still feel sad some days, especially if you're also dealing with other mental health conditions or have other difficult things going on in your life. I'm not asking you to smile through the pain. Crying is okay.

Happiness 24-7 is not the goal. That's unrealistic.

Self-acceptance is the goal. Fulfillment is the goal. Real life is the goal.

Most of all, full-on battle armor against eating disorders must be our goal. Because an eating disorder will keep leeching away your happiness until all that's left is a shell of who you are.

Don't make other people your enemy.

Make the eating disorder your enemy instead.

EXERCISE: YOUR FAVORITE MEMORIES

Make a list of your favorite five memories. How many of them are from when you were actively engaging in your eating disorder? Do they involve food in a healthy way or an obsessive way? Are you with other people in these memories or alone?

EXERCISE: STRENGTHENING RELATIONSHIPS

What three things can you do in the next week to strengthen your relationship with someone you're not as close to anymore? How will you react if that person pushes you away or gets angry?

CHAPTER 24
Clothes Shopping and Clothes Sizes

Clothing shopping: Don't let a tag determine your worth

CLOTHES SHOPPING IS hard for pretty much everyone. Clothes shopping is *especially* hard if you feel as if everyone is looking at you or judging your body or your clothes.

Of course, people probably *aren't* judging you at all. They're not really looking at you. (Well, some might be, but they should find more important things to concentrate on. Like their own lives, maybe. School? Homework? Brushing their teeth? Dental hygiene is always a good idea.) But, depending on who your friends or classmates are, it might feel as if people want to know what size you wear, especially when they're always talking about fitting into things themselves.

If you know that your friends all wear small-sized clothes,

it might be hard to accept, never mind proudly proclaim, that you wear larger-sized clothes—and that there's nothing wrong with that.

If you gain weight as you recover from an eating disorder, it might be difficult to realize that your old clothes may not fit anymore. That you're not whatever size you used to be anymore. That your body is growing and you're bigger than before.

Developing a positive body image is hard, especially as you're learning to love—or at least accept—your body. Especially in a society that assigns values to certain clothing sizes. In our culture, small equals good and large equals bad, especially for women and feminine people.

Sizes aren't consistent

Clothing sizes shift and change depending on the manufacturer, the store, even the year! The pants in my closet are three different sizes. They all fit my body. My body doesn't change each time I put on a different pair of pants. The pants all look the same, too.

It's only the number that's different. The number that someone else attached to the pants. A number based on manufacturing, design, and marketing decisions that someone else made.

These sizing differences are especially notable in

women's clothing. Some brands practice vanity sizing, where they lower the number on a clothing label to make women feel better about themselves.

In a 2016 YouTube video, "Size Inconsistency + Body Positivity—The True Story," fashion designer Mallorie Dunn explains how sizing differences happen, even within brands. Big clothing companies don't actually design or manufacture their products themselves. Instead, they buy different clothing lines from different design houses, who all have their own fit standards, who all have their own size charts, and who all use different manufacturers.[99]

So it makes sense that I have three different sizes in my closet, especially if they were made by three different companies! A size 6 pair of jeans can vary in the waistband by as much as six inches.[100]

Try not to look at tags in the store. Cut them out once you get the clothes home. You don't have to fit your clothes. Let your clothes fit you. The right-now you. The *you* you are becoming.

Where did clothing sizes come from?

When women made their own clothes or had them made, no sizes were necessary. Clothes were made from each individual measurement. But in the twentieth century, as women started to buy ready-made clothes off the rack, a standard system of sizing became necessary so clothes would fit properly, regardless of where they were bought. In the 1930s, statisticians measured fifteen thousand women, hoping to come up with a sizing system based on the "Average American Woman." They failed. In 1958, though, the National Bureau of Standards used that data, along with the measurements of military women who served in World War II, to come up with "Body Measurements for the Sizing of Women's Patterns and Apparel." The commercial standard based women's sizes on the bust, with all other measurements derived from the proportions of an hourglass figure.[101]

Obviously, all women do not have this same figure, so you can already see where problems began to arise.

The government updated the sizing charts in 1970, but it was apparent that the original data was flawed and not representative of the average woman at all. First off, researchers had left out nonwhite women altogether. Because a small sum had been paid to the volunteer subjects in the 1930s, the measurements were likely skewed toward the poor and malnourished. The military women were, on average, fitter than the general population. The sizing standard became voluntary, and in 1983 it was dropped entirely.

That's when vanity sizing began, and sizes started shifting. One example of changing sizes is that a size 8 today is the same as a size 16 from 1958.[102]

Finding clothes that fit your body and your budget

Recovery and a changing body shape can be complicated by the fact that we have to actually clothe and cover our bodies. Too often, we look at clothing as something we have to "fit into." There is a size that we want to wear, and we work on our body until we can fit into that size. But what happens if we change our thinking and flip these statements around?

What if instead of finding clothes that we can fit *into*, we look for clothes that fit our bodies?

This statement can be revolutionary because instead of changing our bodies, we now have to change the clothes. It makes the *clothes* "bad"—or, rather, wrong for us— instead of our *bodies* being "bad."

In recovery, or as you give up dieting and embrace your natural body shape, you may go through a body shift. You may go through *multiple* body shifts and through multiple sizes.

That's where it gets tricky, because clothes cost money! This financial piece can be a real concern, especially since you need something to wear as you travel from your "now" size to your "recovered" size. (Which, remember, may change eventually, too! You will not be the same size forever. Bodies change in different stages of life, and this is totally normal. What's not normal is to stay the same exact weight forever.)

During recovery, many people embrace sweatpants,

yoga pants, and leggings—clothes that have elastic waist-bands rather than buttons, zippers, and stiff waistbands. A constricting feeling around the waist can be triggering for some people as they gain weight. Skirts and dresses without zippers often work for the same reason, and people can also use adjustable belts to deal with a shifting figure.

To save money while dealing with the need for new clothes, many people swap clothing with their friends. (In this case, you should make sure that seeing your old clothes alongside other people's won't make you feel bad.) Put aside a bunch of clothes that you either don't wear anymore, that don't fit, or were from a time when you engaged in disordered behaviors. If your friends do the same, you can all get together and mix and match for a brand-new wardrobe.

Many department stores have cheaper prices than boutique stores, and secondhand and consignment shops are often full of less-expensive finds. If you don't like the thrift store offerings near you, you can talk to a parent or guardian about helping you look for affordable secondhand clothes on resale and consignment websites like eBay, Poshmark, Vinted, or thredUP.

While there's still not enough affordably priced plus-size fashion, as of 2018, a growing number of retailers and brands do offer stylish, inclusively sized clothes, including: ASOS's Curve and Plus lines, Universal Standard, Torrid, River Island's Big and Tall line, Premme, ModCloth, Target's plus-size section, Old Navy's plus-size section, Forever21+, H&M+, Nordstrom and Nordstrom Rack's plus-size sections, eShakti, Ashley Stewart, Eloquii, RWN by Rawan, MVP Collections, Astra Signature, and others. (Note: These brands are mostly geared toward juniors or adult sizes, but Old Navy, H&M, JCPenney, Kohl's, and Gap have plus-size sections in kids' sizes.) While many of these brands are online-only and there still aren't enough stores that offer inclusive sizing, there's a growing number of options for a range of bodies.

Clothes can hold you back

It's a great idea for people struggling with body image and disordered eating to get rid of the clothes they wore when they had disordered eating. Because it's those clothes, above all, that contribute to the discomfort, both bodily and emotional. Wear sweatpants! Stretchy leggings! Wear sweatshirts and loose T-shirts for a while, until you can buy waistbands that fit your body.

I might wear a different size from some people, but here's another way to look at it: Some people wear a different size from mine, too. They are different. I am different. So why *shouldn't* we look different and dress differently? Your clothing size is just a number, no matter what Hollywood or your mother or that annoying lady on that talk show says.

One action that really helped me when I was recovering was to cut the clothing tags out of my clothes. This simple step is so helpful to those in recovery—it would most likely be helpful for those who don't even *have* eating disorders!

The number on that tag is simply that—a number. The number on that tag doesn't hold any indication of how hard you're working at recovery. It doesn't say how strong and courageous you are or how kind and helpful. It is a number that someone else created.

You are the one creating your life now. And *you* do not need to be defined by a clothing tag.

All you need is an outfit that fits your body and makes you feel comfortable and confident.

So get those clothing tags out of your sight. Force those numbers out of your head. Let your body be what it is and do what it needs to do to get healthy.

On your journey to recovery or to a healthy body image, you might have to gain weight. If you wanted to lose weight, you might have to give up that goal. You might have to buy new clothes. Your body may feel different, and your clothes may feel different. But this is not a failure, just as it's not a failure to wear a different size from your friends' sizes.

Don't want to be *them*. Want to be *you*. My life has been so much more complete since I realized that it's okay to be me. It's important to be me. It's crucial to be me. Once you accept that fact, *that's* when you can change the world.

Weight is a number. Size is a number. Clothes are fabric. *You* are a person.

Be you.

EXERCISE: DON'T LOOK AT TAGS

Ask an adult to help you cut the tags out of your clothes. Or when you get a new pair of pants/shirt/whatever, don't look at the tags. How does it feel to wear that item? Do you judge yourself less if you don't look at the tags first?

EXERCISE: WHAT TO DO WITH OLD CLOTHES

If you find that you're getting rid of a lot of clothes, think about what you should do with those clothes. If you need money, maybe an adult can help you sell your old clothes at a local consignment store. Maybe you can donate your old clothes to a local charity or thrift shop. You can even organize a clothing swap among your friends as a low-cost way for all of you to get new clothes.

CHAPTER 25
Body Image and Body Changes

The pressure to have the "right" body

IT'S EASY TO believe that if the tag on our jeans is a certain number, if the digits on the scale are below a certain number, if your body looks a particular way—a *very particular* way, one that is narrowly defined by some person or some group we can't even identify!—you win. You won't be laughed at. You'll get to sit at the cool table and have tons of friends. Your parents won't criticize you.

Life in the "right"-sized body is supposed to be amazing.

And if you aren't that magical sparkly size right *now*, we're told life *will* be amazing once you reach that size and look exactly the "right" way.

Life will be perfect then.

It will be. It should be. *It has to be.*

Nope. It won't.

You'll have the same problems and the same fears and the same life no matter what size clothes you wear. Your problems won't shrink as you do. Your confidence won't soar along with your muscle tone.

Dieting doesn't help

In fact, the more obsessed you become with food, the more problems you'll have and the lower your confidence and self-esteem will be. Because you'll still have the same problems as before. But now you'll have even *more* problems. You'll turn inward, to your world of disordered eating, as the life you thought would be yours slips further away.

Strangely enough—at least it's strange in the eyes of our diet-obsessed culture—the only solution to this unhappiness is to stop obsessing about weight and stop shaming yourself about the food you eat or the amount of activity you do. For many people—including many people struggling with anorexia—this means gaining weight. For others, this means making peace with the body you have and not obsessing about the future possibility of weight gain. *This* is how you get healthy. *This* is how you reclaim your life.

Your body is supposed to change throughout your life

It often seems as if gaining weight is a sin. As if "putting on a few pounds" during the holidays is the worst thing ever. As if buying a bigger pants size is something to hide. For those assigned female at birth, growing breasts and hips and curves may feel uncomfortable and wrong, as if you now take up too much space in the world. If people make comments about what your body looks like and how it might be changing, those comments can be hard to deal with. But that doesn't mean that anything is wrong with your body. The society that allows these comments is at fault.

Maybe your body is changing now. Maybe you hate it, especially if many of your classmates aren't developing in the same way. Maybe you wish that you had a different body altogether.

It's not wrong to feel that way. Of course body changes feel strange! Any amount of change is an adjustment, whether it's breaking in a new pair of shoes, moving to a new town, or having your body basically transform into a new and different shape.

And that's what puberty feels like sometimes: as if you're morphing into a different person. Your body takes up more room than it used to. You carry yourself differently. You look and feel wrong in clothes you used to love. People may even treat you differently, something that can feel uncomfortable, especially when you feel like the same person on the inside.

Our bodies change, just as *we* change in so many other areas of our lives.

Change is a part of life, though, even though it often feels scary. But change can be good, too! If we stayed the same our entire lives, we wouldn't learn new things. We wouldn't test ourselves and strive and achieve.

We wouldn't feel the sense of accomplishment and peace that comes with beating an eating disorder and accepting ourselves.

Your body knows where it's meant to be, where your weight and your shape are supposed to settle. Just as you have a set eye color and a set number of teeth in your mouth, your body has a weight range where it's most comfortable, as I have mentioned throughout this book. As hard as I worked to diet and count calories and exercise my body into a different shape, it kept fighting back. I kept having to work harder and harder. And that work made me more and more miserable.

It's okay to feel uncomfortable with your body

My body is where it's supposed to be now. I wear a size different from what I wore before I had an eating disorder, but that's okay. I'm older now. I'm not a kid anymore, so my body isn't supposed to look like a kid's body. I'm also happier now.

I wasn't happy at first, though.

At first, it felt awful to grow out of my clothes, and I kept looking in the mirror to see what my body looked like. People call this "body checking," which is basically a way of reassuring yourself that you're not getting "too big." That your body isn't "changing too fast." That's it's not "wrong."

Your body *isn't* wrong, but it might *feel* wrong. It might feel wrong for a long time. For me, and for many sufferers of eating disorders, bad body image was the last symptom to disappear. Even when I had no problems eating according to my meal plan and was exercising appropriately, I didn't like how my body looked some days. I still felt awful about myself because my body was growing.

It's never easy, but it gets better

Honestly, some days I still feel completely different from how I look—my self-image doesn't match my actual weight or appearance. Lots of recovered people feel that way sometimes. Lots of "normal" people do, too. The difference is that now I can deal with these emotions. I realize how I feel, tell myself that my feelings are irrational, and try to figure out what I'm really worried about. If all else fails, I distract myself until the feeling passes.

Bad body image *does* pass. It eventually goes away. You just have to wait it out. Wait out the discomfort. Wait out the pain and the fear.

Meghan Kacmarcik, an anti-diet dietitian at New Moon Nutrition, told me about her own experience gaining weight while recovering from an eating disorder: "I tried to approach all these changes with curiosity rather than judgment, which was my natural response to any body changes. Growing out of clothes and not having any clothes that truly fit you but not wanting to buy more in case you gain more—that's a challenge for sure. It's amazing how much better a well-fitting pair of pants and bra will make you feel. During that period, I tried to stick to loose, flowy clothes and shop at thrift stores so I wasn't spending all my money on things that would only fit for a few weeks. Once my weight stabilized, it felt so good to rebuild my wardrobe with things I actually felt good in, not what I thought I 'should' wear."[103]

Now that she's not so obsessed with her body, Kacmarcik added, her life is so much bigger than before: "For so long, I thought my body was the most interesting thing about me, and it is not! It's really quite boring compared to my kindness, compassion, intelligence, and more."

EXERCISE: BODY CHECKING

Pick a day and make a note every time you check your body in twenty-four hours. Why do you keep touching or looking at your body? What does this do for you? Is it reassuring? Are you comparing yourself with others? Does it make you feel bad about yourself? Does anything in your environment cause it (seeing a mirror, being in a certain situation, hearing someone else talk about their body)? How can you put barriers in place so you don't check so much?

CHAPTER 26
But Will I Relapse?

Will I relapse?

IF YOU HAVE recovered from an eating disorder, this is one question you may have been asking yourself throughout this entire book. It's something I wondered a lot when I read and heard advice about recovery in my early days of trying to get better:

Okay, so you're telling me to trust the process and trust my body and gain weight and realize that I'm a good person regardless of my body? You're telling me that all this anxiety and discomfort will be worth it? That recovering will make me happy? You're telling me to leap and everything will be okay? Promise? Do you promise that everything will be okay? That I won't have any more problems ever?

I had to know that everything would turn out perfectly

before I committed myself to recovery, before I let myself take that leap. I needed that answer—but no one could give it to me. No one could tell me that life would be perfect someday.

Sometimes you'll struggle, and that's okay

I can't promise you that life will be perfect someday, either. After you recover, you will still have problems. Your life will still be hard. The difference will be that you won't have an eating disorder getting in the way of that life anymore. You won't be planning your day around your disordered eating or your exercise. You won't be hiding your bingeing and purging from the world.

You'll have ups and downs and in-betweens. You'll be able to participate more fully in life.

I remember that when I was in treatment for the first time, we had a college student come to speak to us. She had suffered from an eating disorder for years and was finally recovered. She talked about her journey and the struggles she'd had. Then she said something that I've always remembered. She said that when she was sick, *she'd* heard a speaker, too. That she'd been told that even if the world of her eating disorder seemed dark and bleak, "on the other side, there's only flowers." This speaker seemed to love that image. She proclaimed how much it had inspired her to think of herself living in a dirty swamp or a desolate wasteland—and then realizing that recovery would be this brilliant multi-colored garden paradise.

That thought helped her get better.

That thought bothered me, though. It still does, as lovely as a land of flowers sounds. It reminds me of the scene in *The Wizard of Oz* when Dorothy and her companions frolic through a field of poppies, the Emerald City glittering green in the distance. They're happy and excited. They're almost there. It's beautiful.

Then they're tired. They're falling asleep, seduced by the poppies into dreamland.

That's what the "there's only flowers" image is to me: all glitter and no substance. It hypnotizes you into focusing on this mirage in the distance and ignoring reality. Ignoring the distance you still have to cover before you reach your own Emerald City. Distance that makes you tired. That makes you consider giving up when things aren't so perfect.

Recovery isn't a smooth yellow brick road. It's filled with potholes and weeds and big nasty roots that want to trip you. It *isn't* only flowers, and when I heard that speaker say that so many years ago, I think I already knew this on some instinctive level. Certain aspects of my life had led me to develop an eating disorder. On some levels, the entire *world* has an eating disorder. So why should I expect these difficulties to stop once I was "all better"?

I don't command the world. I can't snap my fingers and make my surroundings burst into bloom. All I could do—all I can *still* do—is choose how I respond to the world and what choices I make every day. Sometimes I'll see flowers. Sometimes I'll see weeds. But it's my choice whether or not to pick up my spade and my hoe and my gardening gloves and work to make my patch of soil the best environment for me.

It will be the same for you. Whether you enter treatment with a professional or not, you will have a million little choices to make once you make that first *big* choice—the choice to finally recover and to reclaim your healthy relationship with food, exercise, and your body. You may hear society and the media telling you certain things. You may have friends and family telling you certain things. You will see them perform actions and eat (or not eat) things that go directly against what you know *you're* supposed to do to stay healthy.

You will have to do the opposite.

You will have to ignore them.

You will have to stand up to your friends and tell them that they aren't helping you or that spending time with them isn't healthy at this point in your life.

You will have to tell your family and your therapist (if you have one) when you've slipped up.

You will be disappointed in yourself. You will *want* to engage in disordered eating or exercise.

You may even act on that urge.

Preventing lapses from becoming relapses

You might relapse. I did. I relapsed a bunch of times. Relapse rates for anorexia nervosa range from 9 percent to 65 percent, with the highest risk in the first four to twelve months after treatment.[104] In a 2007 study, 47 percent of women with bulimia relapsed over a five-year period.[105]

Relapse happens. And relapse stinks, both because your obsessions come rolling back *and* because you have to go through the whole recovery process again. The whole long, hard slog of it.

You can fight back from a relapse, though. If you have a moment where you fall back on disordered eating or purging or excessive exercise, you don't have to let that one moment become a series of behaviors. That's the difference between a "lapse" and a "relapse."

A lapse is a one-time thing. A lapse isn't ideal, of course, but a lapse will probably happen. No single person enters recovery and recovers "perfectly." Believing that you will do everything perfectly is just going to set yourself up for failure. That's what happened to me at first. When I had lapses, I was so ashamed of them that I didn't tell anyone. I kept them a secret.

Eating disorders love secrets. Secrets are fuel for eating disorders. They make eating disorders stronger. Because when you don't tell anyone about a lapse, you won't get the help you need. When you don't get the help you need, you'll have another lapse.

And before you know it, that one lapse will turn into a relapse.

Talk about your lapses. Admit that you're struggling. Be open and honest. It's hard to admit that you're struggling, but it's the only way to move forward. It's part of the work that needs to be done. The tools that you've learned in this book and talking with a therapist or in a support group will help, too.

Learn who you are and what you like. Practice being assertive. Use your coping skills. Confront the societal messages and situations that may lead you to start worrying about your body again.

These skills will be your armor and your weapons against your eating disorder. And you *will* emerge victorious, no matter how hard it is or how long it takes. I believe in you.

Here's the thing: You *will* think about your body. You *will* have to eat. You can't stop doing both. You have a body, and you have to eat to survive. You can't cut food out of your life. You can't ignore your body. (You can remove mirrors and cut out tags, but you will still have a body. It's one of the side effects of being human!)

The world will comment on your body, too. People will comment when you eat differently. When you look bigger or smaller than you used to. When you don't exercise as you used to. People may comment and people may judge these differences. You may (you *will*) judge yourself. Keep going. Step by step, minute by minute, meal by meal, move forward.

You may trip and fall.

You may fall down a hole and have to scramble to get to the surface again.

You may need help to get out of that hole.

Eventually, you will be able to pull yourself out.

You may read this book and reevaluate your relationship with your body and not have a single body image problem ever again. I hope so! That would be wonderful.

It probably won't be like that, though. I'm not saying this to be discouraging. I'm not saying this because I have a psychic prediction that your life will be miserable and awful.

Your life *can* be wonderful. But *everyone's* life has its ups and downs. Everyone's life has low points.

It's okay to "miss" disordered eating or exercise

Sometimes, people in recovery have moments of mourning their eating disorder, even though it made their lives awful in so many ways. Even if being sick feels miserable, your eating disorder *did* have a purpose. It eased your anxiety in times of stress. It gave you something to focus on. It made you feel "special." It made you feel safe.

It's okay if you feel sad and grieve the loss. It's okay to have moments of wanting to be back where you were before. Having an eating disorder can feel simple. It can feel easy in many ways. Eating disorders are made up of routine and numbers and rules. With an eating disorder, you don't have to experience the full spectrum of your emotions. You don't have to deal with hard times. You are in control.

But were you *really* in control? When you feel this sense of loss, it's so important to come back around to this question. You may have *felt* as if you were in control, as if you were managing your body and your exercise and your bingeing and purging just fine. *But were you?* This is when you have to remember the depression and the discomfort that came along with being sick. The isolation and anxiety. The fear. The loss of your social life. The loss of your self.

In times of relapse, in times of mourning and regret, focus on what an eating disorder can steal from you. Focus on what you will gain in recovery. Keep that focus until you don't *need* to focus so much anymore. Until you don't need the reminders of how your life will be better—because you'll already be living it.

There are two schools of thought when it comes to recovery. One is that once you are recovered, then you are *recovered.* You will rarely think about your body again. You won't have any urges to restrict or binge or purge. You will love yourself enough to never engage in your old behaviors. I like the concept of being recovered. Most days I *do* feel recovered.

But I also have mornings when I wake up and feel unhappy with my body. I also have moments of stress when I may have a knee-jerk reaction to go for a long run. That doesn't mean that I'll do anything to harm my recovery, though. That doesn't mean that I'll listen to that whisper in my brain.

That's all it is: a whisper. Those minuscule urges are a reminder of days past, a way that my brain, for whatever reason, with all its unique chemicals and hormones, has chosen to communicate with me in times of stress.

For this reason, I don't always say that I'm recovered. I more often say that I'm "forever recovering." For me, recovery is a journey. It's a way for me to keep learning about myself. To keep learning about what scares me and what worries me. To continue to discover what I like and dislike. When I feel stressed or even the slightest bit tempted to do something that focuses too much on making my body smaller, I know that I need to stop and remember what's important.

You don't have to do anything at all dramatic. You don't have to make a big scene. It can be as little as pausing and asking yourself three key questions:

Am I doing something that's healthy for me?

What is my motivation behind this?

Does this action line up with what I want out of life?

You can ask yourself these questions if you get an urge to listen to your eating disorder, or you can create your own questions. Just make sure to be vigilant. Look out for the potholes up ahead. Being aware and keeping your eyes open lets you avoid those potholes so you can keep moving toward the Emerald City in the distance.

This Emerald City won't be an illusion, though. Your Emerald City can be whatever you want it to be. A world where food is good, where you can eat what you want and enjoy being in your body.

Where it doesn't matter what everyone else is eating because you know what's right for you.

Where you can let your body rest if it wants rest.

Where you don't have to eat the entire box of cookies now. It will be there later. But you *can* eat a few because they're so delicious.

Where you don't have to spend hours in the gym shutting out the world.

Your life is here, waiting for you, ready to welcome you when you close the pages of this book.

You are here now.

I am so proud of you. Life is hard. Body acceptance is hard. But you are dealing with it and facing the world. Even by reading this book, you are announcing that you matter. That your peace of mind matters.

You are unique. There is no one else out there with your strengths, your talents, and your body. You don't have to be like other people. *They* are *already* in the world. Now it's time for you to be here, too. Shine your light. Take up space.

You are enough.

Acknowledgments

THIS BOOK HAS been the work of a lifetime. A lifetime of struggle, growth, and self-love. I could not have written this book—I could not be who I am today—without the difficulties that I went through in my life. Without the people who were beside me during my eating disorder. So first of all, I want to thank my parents. Now that I'm a parent, I can understand how hard it was to see me go through all of this. You were supportive and strong and there with me every step of the way. None of us were perfect, but together, we made it through. Thank you to my brothers, Sean and Michael Clancy, and my extended family. Thank you to the staff of Laurel Hill Inn and Walden Behavioral Care, to Linda MacDonald and Tenley Prince, and to all the wise, sensitive, and determined men and women I met throughout treatment.

Thank you to Jean Feiwel, Christine Barcellona, and Val Otarod. I could not have imagined three more perfect editors to help me through the process of bringing this book to life. Your attention to detail; incisive, sensitive comments; and detailed research leave me in awe.

My deepest appreciation also to my agent, Brianne Johnson. Bri, you are a dynamo, a cheerleader, a sounding board, and a warm hug. Thank you for everything you do.

Thank you to the immensely talented team at Feiwel & Friends, who worked tirelessly to put this book together: Starr Baer, Rebecca Syracuse, Sophie Erb, Raymond Colón, Sherri Schmidt, Erin Siu, Kelsey Marrujo, and Melissa Zar, this book wouldn't be what it is without your talent.

I spoke with and interviewed numerous people over the course of researching and writing this book, each of whom provided vital information and unique perspectives. Thank you to all of them for giving their time, talent, and viewpoints: Michelle; Stephanie Covington Armstrong; Jamie Bushell; Ragen Chastain; Alexis Johnson; Meghan Kacmarcik; Lori Lieberman, MPH, RDN, LDN, CDE; Katie Linden; Katherine Locke; Kyle Lukoff; Sarah M.; Angie Manfredi; Melissa Martini; Shanetta McDonald; Sam J. Miller; Marie Southard Ospina; Mariela Podolski, MD; Rachel Simon; Josée Sovinsky; Virgie Tovar; Andrew Walen; Alithia Skye Zamantakis; and Katie Zeitz.

Thanks also go to Martha Peaslee Levine, MD, who provided a medical reading of this book; Sarah Hollowell, who did a sensitivity read; and Rachel B. Monroe and Holly Harmon, who read an early draft of this book.

I could not navigate this publishing journey without my writer friends: Rachel Simon and the Electric Eighteens debut group kept me sane as I delved into the world of the "post-debut" year. So many thanks and hugs to my "real-life" friends, too, especially Kate Averett, Pam Styles, and Jena DiPinto, who encouraged me throughout the writing of this book.

My heart and all my love go to my husband, Brian, and my daughters, Ellie and Lucy. Brian, you have spent years learning about eating disorders first- and second-hand and never gave up on me. You still deal with my anxious, perfectionist self. You are my best friend and helped me learn to love myself. Ellie and Lucy, you are strong and capable and funny and silly and kind. I am so lucky to be your mother, and the world is so lucky to have you both.

Finally, to you, my readers. You deserve more than a life fighting your body and your mind. The world wants you. It needs you. You are absolutely wonderful. You are perfectly imperfect. You are enough.

SCHOLARSHIP FUNDS FOR TREATMENT

Avalon Hills Foundation

avalonhillsfoundation.org

The Avalon Hills Foundation helps to fund treatment for those who cannot afford it financially, while also providing grants for research and awareness programs about eating disorders.

Kirsten Haglund Foundation

kirstenhaglundfoundation.org

Created by Miss America 2008, this foundation continues Kirsten Haglund's work educating the public about eating disorders, while also providing money for treatment scholarships.

Manna Fund
mannafund.org

A nonprofit organization that provides funds for inpatient, residential, partial hospitalization, and intensive outpatient eating disorder treatment for those with little or no insurance coverage.

Moonshadow's Spirit
moonshadowsspirit.org

Founded in memory of Jennifer Mathiason, this organization gives financial aid on a quarterly basis to those who cannot afford treatment.

Project HEAL
theprojectheal.org

Created in 2008 by two recovering teenagers, Project HEAL raises money for those who cannot afford treatment. Project HEAL also offers support groups, opportunities to get involved in advocacy, and a blog.

RECOMMENDED RESOURCES

Websites and Blogs

NEDA: NATIONAL EATING DISORDERS ASSOCIATION

nationaleatingdisorders.org

800-931-2237

The NEDA Helpline is available Monday–Thursday from 9 a.m. to 9 p.m. eastern time and Friday 9 a.m. to 5 p.m. to give support to those struggling with disordered eating. The website also features a chat option.

ANAD: National Association of Anorexia Nervosa and Associated Disorders

anad.org

630-577-1330

The ANAD Eating Disorders Helpline is open Monday–Friday, 9 a.m. to 5 p.m. central time. The trained helpline staff answers questions about symptoms and provides referrals to therapists and support groups. You can also e-mail for more information about ANAD's services.

MEDA: Multi-Service Eating Disorders Association

medainc.org

617-558-1881

A nonprofit eating disorders organization based in New England, MEDA provides clinical assessments, recovery support groups, and access to further treatment. As part of its education and support mission, it sponsors monthly Hope and Inspiration forums, where recovered individuals share their stories. The stories can be read at www.medainc.org/services/heal/stories-of -recovery/.

Recovery Warriors

recoverywarriors.com

Recovery Warriors features stories, blog posts, poetry, art, and a podcast to help people recovering from depression, anxiety, and eating disorders.

Eating Disorder Hope
eatingdisorderhope.com

This website provides articles on recovery, support, and treatment options and includes links to treatment centers and therapists. It sponsors live online forums and webinars for both sufferers and clinicians and offers blog and video posts about recovery.

Eating Disorder Referral and Information Center
edreferral.com

Here, readers can search for therapists and treatment centers by specific issue and location. The site provides information about eating disorder treatment options throughout the world.

Proud2BMe
proud2bme.org/content/about-us

Created by and made for teens, this online community features blog posts, interviews, and news about body image and self-esteem for girls *and* boys.

TeensHealth
kidshealth.org/en/teens

This online guide provides doctor-approved information on teens' health issues, including mental health, physical health, drugs, and alcohol.

Pacer Center's Teens Against Bullying

pacerteensagainstbullying.org

Created by and for teens, this site discusses bullying, both in person and online, its effects, and ways to address it and take action in daily life.

Scarleteen: Sex Ed for the Real World

scarleteen.com

Scarleteen provides comprehensive, open information about sexuality and relationships for teenagers. It covers gender, sexuality, body image, and sexual health and includes message boards and live chats.

A Mighty Girl

amightygirl.com

This website promotes girl-positive messages with recommendations for books, movies, music, and toys.

National Suicide Prevention Hotline

suicidepreventionlifeline.org

1-800-273-8255

This lifeline provides free, confidential emotional support by trained crisis workers twenty-four hours a day, seven days a week. It also gives crisis and prevention resources for those in distress, for their loved ones, and for professionals.

ThirdwheelED

thirdwheeled.com

In this blog, two queer individuals discuss eating disorders, recovery, and support from their unique perspective.

The Trevor Project

thetrevorproject.org
866-488-7386

The Trevor Project provides crisis intervention and suicide prevention services to lesbian, gay, bisexual, transgender, and questioning young people. Its helpline can be reached twenty-four hours a day and is staffed with trained counselors. The website also provides live chats with counselors, a secure social-networking space for LGBTQ teens, and resources to answer questions about sexual orientation and gender identity.

It Gets Better Project

youtube.com/user/itgetsbetterproject/

A series of YouTube videos created to inspire gay, lesbian, bisexual, and transgender youth that life does get better after adolescence.

Instagram Accounts

@recoverwithmeda
Inspiration and news from the leading eating disorders nonprofit in the northeast United States.

@positivebodyimage
Inspirational quotes and memes about self-esteem and body image.

@projectheal
A nonprofit that raises money to pay for eating disorder treatment, Project HEAL posts inspirational quotes and pictures.

@amypoehlersmartgirls
Smart Girls, cocreated by actress and comedian Amy Poehler, strives to encourage girls to "change the world by being yourself!"

@proud2bmeus
Run by the National Eating Disorders Association staff, this account aims to change society's narrative about bodies and weight.

@i_weigh

Created by actress Jameela Jamil, this account aims to twist the narrative around weight to show how we should actually be measured—by the wonderful qualities we have and the amazing things we do.

Books

HARRIS, ROBIE H. *IT'S PERFECTLY NORMAL: CHANGING BODIES, GROWING UP, SEX, AND SEXUAL HEALTH.* SOMERVILLE, MA: CANDLEWICK, 2014.

A guide for kids, teens, and parents, this book covers questions about sex, puberty, sexual identity, safe Internet use, and mental health.

SCHAEFER, JENNI. *LIFE WITHOUT ED: HOW ONE WOMAN DECLARED INDEPENDENCE FROM HER EATING DISORDER AND HOW YOU CAN TOO.* NEW YORK: MCGRAW-HILL EDUCATION, 2003.

A series of lessons and realizations that came with one woman's breakup with "Ed," the name she gave to her eating disorder. Includes tips and exercises to help you separate from your disease, too.

SCHAEFER, JENNI. *GOODBYE ED, HELLO ME: RECOVER FROM YOUR EATING DISORDER AND FALL IN LOVE WITH LIFE.* NEW YORK: MCGRAW-HILL EDUCATION, 2009.

This sequel to *Life Without Ed* contains more lessons about how to move forward with your life once you have moved past disordered eating and how to reclaim your joy and sense of self again.

Taylor, Julia V. *The Body Image Workbook for Teens: Activities to Help Girls Develop a Healthy Body Image in an Image-Obsessed World.* Oakland, CA: Instant Help, 2014.

A series of exercises and coping strategies for teens to use to deal with low self-esteem, family pressures, the media, friendships, and more.

Wachter, Andrea. *Getting over Overeating for Teens: A Workbook to Transform Your Relationship with Food Using CBT, Mindfulness, and Intuitive Eating.* Oakland, CA: Instant Help, 2016.

A workbook filled with exercises and strategies to help kids and teens deal with overeating and its causes.

Body Positive and Inspirational Fiction and Nonfiction

BELL, CECE. *EL DEAFO*. NEW YORK: ABRAMS, 2014.

A graphic novel memoir in which the author reimagines her childhood hearing loss and Phonic Ear hearing aid as if she were a bunny and her hearing aid gave her superpowers!

BOWLING, DUSTI. *INSIGNIFICANT EVENTS IN THE LIFE OF A CACTUS*. NEW YORK: STERLING CHILDREN'S BOOKS, 2017.

Aven was born with no arms, but she doesn't let her differences stop her, even as she moves across the country with her parents to a western theme park, where she meets new friends and solves a mystery.

COOPER, ABBY. *STICKS AND STONES*. NEW YORK: FARRAR STRAUS GIROUX, 2016.

A magical tale of Elyse, who has the unusual condition of having the names people call her appear on her skin.

DePrince, Michaela. *Taking Flight: From War Orphan to Star Ballerina.* New York: Knopf, 2014.

Michaela DePrince's own account of her journey from an orphanage in Sierra Leone, where her vitiligo was mocked, to her adoption and rise to become a ballerina.

Jennings, Jazz. *Being Jazz: My Life as a (Transgender) Teen.* New York: Crown Books for Young Readers, 2016.

Jazz Jennings's personal account of her life as a transgender girl and the discrimination she has faced and overcome.

Kuklin, Susan. *Beyond Magenta: Transgender Teens Speak Out.* Somerville, MA: Candlewick, 2014.

This book profiles the unique journeys of six transgender individuals. The teens represent a variety of races, ethnicities, and sexual and gender identities.

Murphy, Julie. *Dumplin'.* New York: HarperCollins, 2015.

Willowdean is fat, but that doesn't mean she doesn't love herself. Follow her self-esteem journey as she enters a Texas beauty pageant, gets a boyfriend, and teaches others to love her, too. (This title is young adult and is recommended for older readers.)

Telgemeier, Raina. *Smile.* New York: Graphix, 2010.

Based on the author's childhood, this bright graphic novel tells of one girl's struggle with friends and her body after knocking out her front teeth.

SOURCE NOTES

1. Müller, Bosy-Westphal, and Heymsfield, "Evidence for a Set Point."

2. National Eating Disorders Association, "Eating Disorders in LGBTQ+ Populations."

3. Diemer, et al., "Gender Identity."

4. Goebel-Fabbri, "Diabetes and Eating Disorders."

5. "Psychodynamic Therapy."

6. Beck Institute, "What Is Cognitive Behavior Therapy?"

7. Linehan, "What Is Dialectical Behavior Therapy?"

8. Le Grange and Lock, "Family-Based Treatment."

9. Zamantakis, "My Journey."

10. Alithia Skye Zamantakis, interview by the author, April 25, 2017.

11. Michelle, e-mail message to Val Otarod, March 14, 2018.

12. Stephanie Covington Armstrong, e-mail message to Val Otarod, April 3, 2018.

13. Conason, "Evidence for Intuitive Eating."

14. Lori Lieberman, MPH, RDN, LDN, CDE, interview by the author, May 24, 2017.

15. Sarah M., interview by the author, January 10, 2018.

16. Healthwise, "Type 1 Diabetes."

17. Jones, et al., "Eating Disorders in Adolescent Females."

18. Storrs, "High Body Fat."

19. Bacon, "Health at Every Size."

20. Fabello and Bacon, "11 Reasons."

21. Lieberman interview.

22. Mariela Podolski, MD, interview by author, February 2018.

23. Fothergill, et al., "6 Years After 'The Biggest Loser.'"

24. Mayo Clinic, "Panic Attacks."

25. Schmidt, et al., "Exploring Human Freeze Responses."

26. Roelofs, "Freeze for Action."

27. Walker, "Neurodiversity."

28. American Psychiatric Association, "Autism Spectrum Disorder."

29. Rachel Simon, Facebook direct message to author, May 23, 2017.

30. Katie Linden, e-mail message to author, May 8, 2017.

31. Mayo Clinic, "Generalized Anxiety Disorder."

32. Mayo Clinic, "Social Anxiety Disorder."

33. Mayo Clinic, "Obsessive-Compulsive Disorder."

34. Mayo Clinc, "Post-Traumatic Stress Disorder."

35. Mayo Clinic, "Depression."

36. Mayo Clinic, "Bipolar Disorder."

37. McElroy, et al., "Patients with Bipolar Disorder."

38. Dietz, "Distress Tolerance."

39. Walter, "R.I.D.E. the Wave of Panic."

40. Hall, et al., "Yoga in Outpatient Treatment."

41. National Sleep Foundation, "Teens and Sleep."

42. National Sleep Foundation, "Drowsy Driving vs. Drunk Driving."

43. Michelle, e-mail message to Val Otarod, March 14, 2018.

44. "Getting Started with Mindfulness."

45. Cohen and McDermott, "Who's Fat?"

46. Brown, *Body of Truth*, 10.

47. Chen, "BMI Test of Health"; Tomiyama, et al., "Misclassification of Cardiometabolic Health."

48. Chen, "BMI Test of Health."

49. Katie Zeitz, Facebook direct message to author, November 20, 2017.

50. Baker, "Change Your World."

51. This and the following quotation are from Alexis Johnson, e-mail message to Val Otarod, March 21, 2018.

52. Michelle, e-mail message to Val Otarod, March 14, 2018.

53. Sim, Lebow, and Billings, "Adolescents with a History of Obesity."

54. Lipson and Sonneville, "Eating Disorder Symptoms."

55. Melissa Martini, e-mail message to author, November 21, 2017.

56. Llewellyn, et al., "Finding the Missing Heritability."

57. Marketdata, "U.S. Weight Loss Market."

58. Lang, "Global Box Office."

59. Fletcher, "Fat-Acceptance Movement."

60. This and the following quotation are from Dionne, "Fat Acceptance Activists."

61. This and the following two quotations are from Virgie Tovar, interview by the author, May 9, 2017.

62. Brown, "The Obesity Paradox"; Hughes "The Big Fat Truth"; Flegal, et al., "Mortality with Overweight and Obesity."

63. Arcelus, et al., "Mortality Rates in Anorexia Nervosa"; DeNoon, "Deadliest Psychiatric Disorder: Anorexia."

64. Mayo Clinic, "Anorexia Nervosa" and "Bulimia Nervosa."

65. Angie Manfredi, e-mail message to author, May 21, 2017. Her blog can be found at fatgirlreading.com.

66. This and following quotation are from Ragen Chastain, e-mail message to author, May 22, 2017. Her blog can be found at danceswithfat.wordpress.com.

67. Manfredi interview.

68. Chastain interview.

69. This and the following four quotations are from Alexis Johnson, e-mail message to Val Otarod, March 21, 2018.

70. McDonald, "My 'Quick Fix' Was an Eating Disorder."

71. This and the following quotation are from Shanetta McDonald, e-mail message to author, December 20, 2017.

72. Weidner, "I'm Non-Binary."

73. This and the following quotation are from Katherine Locke, Facebook message to author, April 28, 2017.

74. This and the following two quotations are from Jamie Bushell, e-mail message to author, May 11, 2017.

75. Bushell, "Current Eating Disorder Discourse."

76. This and the following quotation are from Lukoff, "Taking Up Space," 125, 126.

77. Locke interview.

78. Wolf, *The Beauty Myth*, 7–8.

79. Alpert, "Teenage Boys."

80. This and the following two quotations are from Sam J. Miller, e-mail message to author, Feb. 2018.

81. Andrew Walen, interview by the author, April 28, 2017.

82. Hudson, et al., "Prevalence and Correlates of Eating Disorders."

83. Trevor Project, "Eating Disorders Among LGBTQ Youth"

84. Crouse, "Adam Rippon."

85. Sachs, "Chance Encounter with First Lady," Jan. 10, 2017.

86. Winslet, "A Heavenly Creature."

87. Tina Fey, quoted in Young, *Secret Thoughts*, 134–5.

88. Streep, interview by Burns.

89. Edwards, "Quotes on Impostor Syndrome."

90. Owens, "Beyonce, Colorism"; "Why Do Magazines Lighten Black Faces?"

91. Kuo, "Socially Accepted Beauty Ideals."

92. Dove, "Evolution."

93. BBC, "France Bans Extremely Thin Models."

94. This and the following three quotations are from Michelle, e-mail message to Val Otarod, March 14, 2018.

95. UNC Health Care, "Genetic Locus."

96. This and the following three quotations are from Marie Southard Ospina, e-mail message to author, Feb. 2018.

97. Williams, "The Agony of Instagram."

98. Fardouly, "Appearance Comparisons."

99. Dunn, "Size Inconsistency."

100. Dockterman, "One Size Fits None."

101. Stampler, "Bizarre History."

102. Ingraham, "Absurdity of Clothing Sizes."

103. This and the following quotation are from Meghan Kacmarcik RDN, LD, e-mail message to author, May 30, 2017.

104. "Tackling Relapse."

105. Grilo, et al., "Natural Course of Bulimia Nervosa."

SELECTED BIBLIOGRAPHY

A.D.A.M. "Eating Disorders." University of Maryland Medical Center. Accessed Feb. 21, 2018. www.umm.edu/health/medical/reports/articles/eating-disorders.

Alpert, Emily. "Eating Disorders Plague Teenage Boys, Too." *Los Angeles Times*. June 13, 2013. articles.latimes.com/2013/jun/13/local/la-me-boys-eating-disorders-20130614.

American Psychiatric Association. "Diagnostic Criteria for 299.00 Autism Spectrum Disorder." *Diagnostic and Statistical Manual*, 5th ed. Arlington, VA: American Psychiatric Association, 2013, at Centers for Disease Control and Prevention. Accessed Feb. 20, 2018. www.cdc.gov/ncbddd/autism/hcp-dsm.html.

Arcelus, Jon, Alex J. Mitchell, Jackie Wales, and Søren Nielsen. "Mortality Rates in Patients with Anorexia Nervosa and Other Eating Disorders: A Meta-Analysis of 36 Studies." *Archives of General Psychiatry* 68, no. 7 (July 2011): 724–731. doi.org/10.1001/archgenpsychiatry.2011.74.

Armstrong, Stephanie Covington. *Not All Black Girls Know How to Eat: A Story of Bulimia*. Chicago: Chicago Review Press, 2009.

Bacon, Linda. "Health at Every Size." haescommunity.com/.

———. *Health at Every Size: The Surprising Truth About Your Weight*. Dallas: BenBella Books, 2010.

Baker, Jes. "Change Your World, Not Your Body—The Social Impact of Body Love." TEDx Talk filmed May 2014 in Tucson, AZ. July 14, 2014. YouTube video, 16:27. youtu.be/iSjwdN9vW0g.

BBC News. "France Bans Extremely Thin Models." May 6, 2017. www.bbc.com/news/world
-europe-39821036.

Beck Institute for Cognitive Behavior Therapy. "What Is Cognitive Behavior Therapy (CBT)?"
Accessed Feb. 20, 2018. www.beckinstitute.org/get-informed/what-is-cognitive-therapy.

Beil, Laura. "More Men Are Developing Eating Disorders: Why Are We Treating It as Only a
Women's Disease?" *STAT.* Dec. 28, 2016. www.statnews.com/2016/12/28/male-eating
-disorders/.

Body Image Therapy Center. thebodyimagecenter.com.

Brown, Harriet. *Body of Truth: How Science, History, and Culture Drive Our Obsession with
Weight—and What We Can Do About It.* Boston: Da Capo Press, 2015.

———. "The Obesity Paradox: Scientists Now Think That Being Overweight Can Protect Your
Health." *Quartz.* Nov. 17, 2015. qz.com/550527/obesity-paradox-scientists-now-think-that
-being-overweight-is-sometimes-good-for-your-health/.

Bushell, Jamie. "How Current Eating Disorder Discourse Fails the LGBTQ Community. And How
We Can Change That." *HuffPost.* Jan. 24, 2017. www.huffingtonpost.com/entry/how
-current-eating-disorder-discourse-fails-the-lgbtq_us_5975e0fce4b0f1feb89b44e7.

———, ed. *ThirdwheelED: Two Queer Perspectives on Eating Disorder Recovery* (blog).
thirdwheeled.com.

Center for Eating Disorders at Sheppard Pratt. "What Causes an Eating Disorder?" Accessed
Feb. 21, 2018. eatingdisorder.org/eating-disorder-information/underlying-causes.

Chastain, Ragen. *Dances with Fat* (blog). danceswithfat.wordpress.com.

Chen, Angus. "If BMI Is the Test of Health, Many Pro Athletes Would Flunk." NPR. Feb. 4, 2016.
www.npr.org/sections/health-shots/2016/02/04/465569465/.

Clark, Shelby. "Are Eating Disorders More Prevalent in the LGBT Community?" Pride Source.
March 13, 2014. pridesource.com/article/65073-2/.

Cohen, Elizabeth, and Anne McDermott. "Who's Fat? New Definition Adopted." CNN. June 17,
1998. www.cnn.com/HEALTH/9806/17/weight.guidelines/.

Conason, Alexis. "The Evidence for Intuitive Eating." *Psychology Today.* June 27, 2014. www
.psychologytoday.com/blog/eating-mindfully/201406/the-evidence-intuitive-eating.

Cooper, Debra M. "Twin Studies Reveal Eating Disorder Connection." Eating Disorder Hope.
Jan. 4, 2016. www.eatingdisorderhope.com/blog/twin-studies-reveal-eating-disorder
-connection.

Crouse, Karen. "Adam Rippon on Quiet Starvation in Men's Figure Skating." *New York Times*. Feb. 13, 2018. nyti.ms/2BUZ0bP.

DeNoon, Daniel J. "Deadliest Psychiatric Disorder: Anorexia." WebMD. July 12, 2011. www .webmd.com/mental-health/eating-disorders/anorexia-nervosa/news/20110711 /deadliest-psychiatric-disorder-anorexia.

Diemer, Elizabeth W., Julia D. Grant, Melissa A. Munn-Chernoff, David A. Patterson, Alexis E. Duncan. "Gender Identity, Sexual Orientation, and Eating-Related Pathology in a National Sample of College Students." *Journal of Adolescent Health* 57, no. 2 (August 2015): 144–149. doi.org/10.1016/j.jadohealth.2015.03.003.

Dietz, Lisa. "Distress Tolerance." DBT Self Help. www.dbtselfhelp.com/html/distress_tolerance1 .html.

Dionne, Evette. "Fat Acceptance Activists Explain Why Body Positivity Is Becoming Meaningless." Revelist. Jan. 24, 2017. www.revelist.com/ideas/fat-acceptance-body -positivity/6632.

Dockterman, Eliana. "One Size Fits None: Inside the Fight to Take Back the Fitting Room." *Time*. Accessed Feb. 21, 2018. time.com/how-to-fix-vanity-sizing.

Dove. Dove Self-Esteem Project. www.dove.com/us/en/dove-self-esteem-project.html.

———. "Evolution." Directed by Tim Piper. Oct. 2, 2006. YouTube video, 1:14. youtu.be /iYhCn0jf46U.

Dunn, Mallorie. "Size Inconsistency + Body Positivity—The True Story." May 31, 2016. YouTube video, 16:09. youtu.be/VWvtqdlTvOs.

Edwards, Martha. "16 Celebrity Quotes on Suffering with Impostor Syndrome." *Marie Claire*. Nov. 11, 2016. www.marieclaire.co.uk/entertainment/celebrity-quotes-on-impostor -syndrome-434739.

Fabello, Melissa A., and Linda Bacon. "11 Reasons Your Phony 'Concern' for Fat People's Health Has Got to Stop." Everyday Feminism. Jan. 24, 2016. everydayfeminism.com/2016/01 /concern-trolling-is-bullshit/.

Fardouly, Jasmine, Rebecca T. Pinkus, and Lenny R. Vartanian. "The Impact of Appearance Comparisons Made Through Social Media, Traditional Media, and in Person in Women's Everyday Lives." *Body Image* 20 (March 2017): 31–39. doi.org/10.1016/j.bodyim.2016.11.002.

Felsenthal, Julia. "A Size 2 Is a Size 2 Is a Size 8." Slate. January 25, 2012. http://www.slate .com/articles/arts/design/2012/01/clothing_sizes_getting_bigger_why_our_sizing _system_makes_no_sense_.html.

Flegal, Katherine M., Brian K. Kit, Heather Orpana, and Barry I. Graubard. "Association of All-Cause Mortality with Overweight and Obesity Using Standard Body Mass Index Categories." *JAMA* 309, no. 1 (Jan. 2, 2013): 71–82. doi.org/10.1001/jama.2012.113905.

Fletcher, Dan. "The Fat-Acceptance Movement." *Time*. July 31, 2009. content.time.com/time /nation/article/0,8599,1913858,00.html.

Ford, Zack. "Eating Disorders Significantly More Prevalent Among Transgender People, Study Finds." ThinkProgress. Aug. 4, 2015. thinkprogress.org/eating-disorders-significantly -more-prevalent-among-transgender-people-study-finds-b975cd7bba28/.

Fothergill, Erin, Juen Guo, Lilian Howard, Jennifer C. Kerns, Nicolas D. Knuth, Robert Brychta, Kong Y. Chen, et al. "Persistent Metabolic Adaptation 6 Years After 'The Biggest Loser' Competition." *Obesity* 24, no. 8 (Aug. 2016): 1612–1619. doi.org/10.1002/oby.21538.

"Getting Started with Mindfulness." *Mindful*. Accessed Feb. 20, 2018. www.mindful.org /meditation/mindfulness-getting-started.

Goebel-Fabbri, Ann E. "Diabetes and Eating Disorders." *Journal of Diabetes Science and Technology* 2, no. 3 (May 2008): 530–532. doi.org/10.1177/193229680800200326.

Grilo, Carlos M., Maria E. Pagano, Andrew E. Skodol, Charles A. Sanislow, Thomas H. McGlashan, John G. Gunderson, and Robert L. Stout. "Natural Course of Bulimia Nervosa and of Eating Disorder Not Otherwise Specified; 5-year Prospective Study of Remissions, Relapses, and the Effects of Personality Disorder Psychopathology." *Journal of Clinical Psychiatry* 68, no. 5 (May 2007): 738–746. Manuscript at www.ncbi.nlm.nih.gov/pmc/articles/PMC2527481/.

Hall, Allison, Nana Ama Ofei-Tenkorang, Jason T. Machan, and Catherine M. Gordon. "Use of Yoga in Outpatient Eating Disorder Treatment: A Pilot Study." *Journal of Eating Disorders* 4, no. 38 (Dec. 2016). doi.org/10.1186/s40337-016-0130-2.

Halmi, Katherine A., Federica Tozzi, Laura M. Thornton, Scott Crow, Manfred M. Fichter, Allan S. Kaplan, Pamela Keel, et al. "The Relation Among Perfectionism, Obsessive-Compulsive Personality Disorder and Obsessive-Compulsive Disorder in Individuals with Eating Disorders." *International Journal of Eating Disorders* 38, no. 4 (Dec. 2005): 371–374. doi .org/10.1002/eat.20190.

Healthwise. "Type 1 Diabetes: Symptoms." WebMD. www.webmd.com/diabetes/type-1 -diabetes-guide/type-1-diabetes-symptoms#1.

Hudson, James I., Eva Hiripi, Harrison G. Pope Jr., and Ronald C. Kessler. "The Prevalence and Correlates of Eating Disorders in the National Comorbidity Survey Replication." *Biological Psychiatry* 61, no. 3 (Feb. 1, 2007): 348–358. Manuscript at www.ncbi.nlm.nih.gov/pmc /articles/PMC1892232/.

Hughes, Virginia. "The Big Fat Truth." *Nature*. May 22, 2013. doi.org/10.1038/497428a.

Human Rights Campaign. "Sexual Orientation and Gender Identity Definitions." Accessed Feb. 9, 2018. www.hrc.org/resources/sexual-orientation-and-gender-identity-termi nology-and-definitions.

Ingraham, Christopher. "The Absurdity of Women's Clothing Sizes, in One Chart." *Washington Post*. Aug. 11, 2015. wapo.st/1lWz5rT.

Jones, Jennifer M., Margaret L. Lawson, Denis Daneman, Marion P. Olmsted, and Gary Rodin. "Eating Disorders in Adolescent Females with and Without Type 1 Diabetes: Cross Sectional Study." *BMJ: British Medical Journal* 320, no. 7249 (June 10, 2000): 1563–1566. Reprinted at www.ncbi.nlm.nih.gov/pmc/articles/PMC27398/.

Kacmarcik, Meghan. *New Moon Nutrition* (blog). newmoonrd.com/blog/.

Kaye, Walter H., Catherine G. Greeno, Howard Moss, John Fernstrom, Madelyn Fernstrom, Lisa R. Lilenfeld, Theodore E. Weltzin, and J. John Mann. "Alterations in Serotonin Activity and Psychiatric Symptoms After Recovery from Bulimia Nervosa." *Archives of General Psychiatry* 55, no. 10 (Oct. 1998): 927–935. doi.org/10.1001/archpsyc.55.10.927.

Konstantinovsky, Michelle. "Eating Disorders Don't Discriminate." Slate. March 20, 2014. www .slate.com/articles/double_x/doublex/2014/03/eating_disorders_and_women_of _color_anorexia_and_bulimia_are_not_just_white.html.

Kuo, Rachel. "4 Ways Our Socially Accepted Beauty Ideals Are Racist." Everyday Feminism. May 8, 2017. everydayfeminism.com/2017/05/beauty-ideals-racist.

Lang, Brent. "Global Box Office Hits Record $38.6 Billion in 2016 Even as China Slows Down." *Variety*. March 22, 2017. variety.com/2017/film/news/box-office-record-china-1202013961/.

Lavender, Jason M., and James E. Mitchell. "Eating Disorders and Their Relationship to Impulsivity." *Current Treatment Options in Psychiatry* 2, no. 4 (Dec. 2015): 394–401. doi .org/10.1007/s40501-015-0061-6.

Le Grange, Daniel, and James Lock. "Family-Based Treatment of Adolescent Anorexia Nervosa: The Maudsley Approach." Maudsley Parents. Accessed Feb. 20, 2018. www.mauds leyparents.org/whatismaudsley.html.

Lichenstein, Shira. "Riding the Wave: DBT and Distress Tolerance." *Erika's Lighthouse: A Beacon of Hope for Adolescent Depression* (blog). July 26, 2016. www.erikaslighthouse.org/blog /riding-wave-dbt-distress-tolerance.

Linehan, Marsha. "What Is Dialectical Behavior Therapy (DBT)?" Behavioral Tech. Accessed Feb. 20, 2018. behavioraltech.org/resources/whatisdbt.cfm.

Lipson, S. K., and K. R. Sonneville. "Eating Disorder Symptoms Among Undergraduate and Graduate Students at 12 U.S. Colleges and Universities." *Eating Behaviors* 24 (Jan. 2017): 81–88. doi.org/10.1016/j.eatbeh.2016.12.003.

Llewellyn, C. H., M. Trzaskowski, R. Plomin, and J. Wardle. "Finding the Missing Heritability in Pediatric Obesity: The Contribution of Genome-Wide Complex Trait Analysis." *International Journal of Obesity* 37 (March 26, 2013): 1506–1509. doi.org/10.1038/ijo.2013.30.

Lukoff, Kyle. "Taking Up Space." In *Gender Outlaws: The Next Generation*, edited by Kate Bornstein and S. Bear Bergman, 122–127. Berkeley, CA: Seal Press, 2010.

Manfredi, Angie. *Fat Girl, Reading* (blog). www.fatgirlreading.com.

Marketdata Enterprises. "U.S. Weight Loss Market Worth $66 Billion." News release. May 4, 2017. www.webwire.com/ViewPressRel.asp?aId=209054.

Mayo Clinic. "Anorexia Nervosa: Symptoms & Causes." Feb. 20, 2018. www.mayoclinic.org /diseases-conditions/anorexia/symptoms-causes/syc-20353591.

———. "Bipolar Disorder: Symptoms & Causes." Jan. 31, 2018. www.mayoclinic.org/diseases -conditions/bipolar-disorder/symptoms-causes/syc-20355955.

———. "Bulimia Nervosa: Symptoms & Causes." Aug. 23, 2017. www.mayoclinic.org/diseases -conditions/bulimia/symptoms-causes/syc-20353615.

———. "Depression (Major Depressive Disorder): Symptoms & Causes." Feb. 3, 2018. www .mayoclinic.org/diseases-conditions/depression/symptoms-causes/syc-20356007.

———. "Generalized Anxiety Disorder: Symptoms & Causes." Oct. 13, 2017. www.mayoclinic.org /diseases-conditions/generalized-anxiety-disorder/symptoms-causes/syc-20360803.

———. "Obsessive-Compulsive Disorder (OCD): Symptoms & Causes." Sept. 17, 2016. www .mayoclinic.org/diseases-conditions/obsessive-compulsive-disorder/symptoms -causes/syc-20354432.

———. "Panic Attacks and Panic Disorder: Symptoms & Causes." May 19, 2015. www .mayoclinic.org/diseases-conditions/panic-attacks/symptoms-causes/syc-20376021.

———. "Post-Traumatic Stress Disorder (PTSD): Symptoms & Causes." Oct. 25, 2017. www .mayoclinic.org/diseases-conditions/post-traumatic-stress-disorder/symptoms -causes/syc-20355967.

———. "Social Anxiety Disorder (social phobia): Symptoms & Causes." Aug. 29, 2017. www .mayoclinic.org/diseases-conditions/social-anxiety-disorder/symptoms-causes/syc -20353561.

McDonald, Shanetta. "How I Finally Admitted That My 'Quick Fix' Was an Eating Disorder." *Refinery29*. Feb. 29, 2016. www.refinery29.com/african-american-women-bulimia.

McElroy, Susan L., Mark A. Frye, Gerhard Hellemann, Lori Altshuler, Gabriele S. Leverich, Trisha Suppes, Paul E. Keck, Willem A. Nolen, Ralph Kupka, and Robert M. Post. "Prevalence and Correlates of Eating Disorders in 875 Patients with Bipolar Disorder." *Journal of Affective Disorders* 128, no. 3 (Feb. 2011): 191–8. doi.org/10.1016/j.jad.2010.06.037.

Mehanna, Hisham M., Jamil Moledina, and Jane Travis. "Refeeding Syndrome: What It Is and How to Prevent and Treat It." *BMJ: British Medical Journal* 336, no. 7659 (June 26, 2008): 1495–1498. Reprinted at www.ncbi.nlm.nih.gov/pmc/articles/PMC2440847/.

Müller, Manfred J., Anja Bosy-Westphal, and Steven B. Heymsfield. "Is There Evidence for a Set Point That Regulates Human Body Weight?" *F1000 Medicine Reports* 2, no. 59 (Aug. 9, 2010). doi.org/10.3410/M2-59.

National Assocation for Males with Eating Disorders. namedinc.org.

National Eating Disorders Association. "Eating Disorders in LGBTQ+ Populations." Accessed Feb. 9, 2018. www.nationaleatingdisorders.org/eating-disorders-lgbt-populations.

National Sleep Foundation. "Drowsy Driving vs. Drunk Driving: How Similar Are They?" Accessed Feb. 20, 2018. sleepfoundation.org/sleep-topics/drowsy-driving-vs-drunk-driving-how-similar-are-they.

———. "Teens and Sleep." Accessed Feb. 20, 2018. sleepfoundation.org/sleep-topics/teens-and-sleep.

Owens, Ernest. "Beyonce, Colorism, and Why All of This Needs to End in 2013." *HuffPost*. Feb. 14, 2013. www.huffingtonpost.com/ernest-owens/beyonce-colorism-and-why-_b_2687029.html.

"Psychodynamic Therapy." *Psychology Today*. Accessed Feb. 20, 2018. www.psychologytoday.com/therapy-types/psychodynamic-therapy.

Roelofs, Karin. "Freeze for Action: Neurobiological Mechanisms in Animal and Human Freezing." *Philosophical Transactions of the Royal Society B* 372, no. 1718 (April 19, 2017). doi.org/10.1098/rstb.2016.0206.

Sachs, Sarah. "How a Chance Encounter with the First Lady Helped Me Get over Impostor Syndrome." *Washington Post*. Jan. 10, 2017. wapo.st/2i8VO30.

Satter, Ellyn. "Adult Eating and Weight: What Is Normal Eating?" Ellyn Satter Institute. Accessed Feb. 20, 2018. www.ellynsatterinstitute.org/how-to-eat/adult-eating-and-weight/.

Schaefer, Jenni. *Goodbye Ed, Hello Me: Recover from Your Eating Disorder and Fall in Love with Life.* New York: McGraw-Hill Education, 2009.

———. *Life Without Ed: How One Woman Declared Independence from Her Eating Disorder and How You Can Too.* New York: McGraw-Hill Education, 2003.

Schmidt, Norman B., J. Anthony Richey, Michael J. Zvolensky, and Jon K. Maner. "Exploring Human Freeze Responses to a Threat Stressor." *Journal of Behavior Therapy and Experimental Psychiatry* 39, no. 3 (Sept. 2008): 292–304. Manuscript at www.ncbi.nlm.nih.gov/pmc/articles/PMC2489204/.

Shepherd, Leslie. "Underweight People at as High Risk of Dying as Obese People, New Study Finds." St. Michael's Hospital. March 28, 2014. www.stmichaelshospital.com/media/detail.php?source=hospital_news/2014/20140328_hn.

Sim, Leslie A., Jocelyn Lebow, and Marcie Billings. "Eating Disorders in Adolescents with a History of Obesity." *Pediatrics* 132, no. 4 (Oct. 2013): 1026–1030. doi.org/10.1542/peds.2012-3940.

Stampler, Laura. "The Bizarre History of Women's Clothing Sizes." *Time.* Oct. 23, 2014. time.com/3532014/women-clothing-sizes-history.

Storrs, Carina. "High Body Fat, Not BMI, Linked with Higher Death Rate, Study Finds." CNN. March 14, 2016. edition.cnn.com/2016/03/14/health/low-bmi-higher-death-rate/index.html.

Streep, Meryl. Interview by Ken Burns. *USA Weekend*, Dec. 1, 2002. 159.54.226.237/02_issues/021201/021201streep.html.

Sullivan, P. F. "Mortality in Anorexia Nervosa." *American Journal of Psychiatry* 152, no. 7 (July 1995): 1073–1074. doi.org/10.1176/ajp.152.7.1073.

"Tackling Relapse Among Anorexia Nervosa Patients." *Eating Disorders Review* 24, no. 1 (Jan./Feb. 2013). eatingdisordersreview.com/tackling-relapse-among-anorexia-nervosa-patients/.

Thompson, Colleen, Lauren Muhlheim, and Tabitha Farrar. "Set Point Theory." 2014. Mirror Mirror. www.mirror-mirror.org/set.htm.

Tomiyama, A. J., J. M. Hunger, J. Nguyen-Cuu, and C. Wells. "Misclassification of Cardio-metabolic Health When Using Body Mass Index Categories in NHANES 2005–201." *International Journal of Obesity* 40 (Feb. 2016): 883–886. doi.org/10.1038/ijo.2016.17.

Tovar, Virgie. *Lose Hate Not Weight.* www.virgietovar.com.

Trevor Project. "Eating Disorders Among LGBTQ Youth: A 2018 National Assessment." February 28, 2018. https://www.thetrevorproject.org/resources/eating-disorders-among-lgbtq -youth/#sm.003pctcn12r7d1c115b1syzlw1sr5.

UNC Health Care. "For Anorexia Nervosa, Researchers Implicate Genetic Locus on Chromosome 12." News release. May 12, 2017. healthtalk.unchealthcare.org/news/2017 /april/for-anorexia-nervosa-researchers-implicate-genetic-locus-on-chromosome-12.

Walker, Nick. "Neurodiversity: Some Basic Terms & Definitions." Neurocosmopolitanism. Sept. 27, 2014. neurocosmopolitanism.com/neurodiversity-some-basic-terms-definitions/.

Waller, Glenn, Tonya Shaw, Caroline Meyer, Michelle Haslam, Rachel Lawson, and Lucy Serpell. "Persistence, Perseveration, and Perfectionism in the Eating Disorders." *Behavioural and Cognitive Psychotherapy* 40, no. 4 (July 2012): 462–473. doi.org/10.1017 /S135246581200015X.

Walter, Linda. "R.I.D.E. the Wave of Panic." *Psychology Today.* Oct. 5, 2011. www.psychologytoday .com/blog/life-without-anxiety/201110/ride-the-wave-panic.

Weidner, Keress. "I'm Non-Binary, and 'Trans-Accessible' Restrooms Should Include Me, Too." GLSEN. Accessed Feb. 9, 2018. www.glsen.org/blog/i'm-non-binary-and-"trans -accessible"-restrooms-should-include-me-too.

"Why Do Magazines Lighten Black Faces?" Daily Beast. Feb. 6, 2015. thebea.st/1zoX16X.

Williams, Alex. "The Agony of Instagram." *New York Times.* Dec. 13, 2013. nyti.ms/2jDWywl.

Winslet, Kate. "A Heavenly Creature Who Breaks All the Formulas." Interview by Lynda Obst. *Interview*, Nov. 2000. filmlover2.tripod.com/interview_mag.htm.

Wolf, Naomi. *The Beauty Myth: How Images of Beauty Are Used Against Women.* New York: HarperCollins, 2002.

Young, Valerie. *The Secret Thoughts of Successful Women: Why Capable People Suffer from the Impostor Syndrome and How to Thrive in Spite of It.* New York: Crown, 2011.

Zamantakis, Alithia Skye. "My Journey to Eating Disorder Treatment as Neither a Man nor Woman." Everyday Feminism. Jan. 7, 2017. everydayfeminism.com/2017/01/eating -disorder-neither-man-woman.

Zimmerman, Mike. "To Hell and Back: The Untold Story of Male Eating Disorders." *Born Fitness.* Jan. 10, 2017. www.bornfitness.com/male-eating-disorders/.